Post45 Vs. The World

Literary Perspectives on the Global Contemporary

Editor

William G. Welty
Rutgers, The State University of New Jersey

Series in Literary Studies

Vernon Press

In the Americas:
Vernon Press
1000 N West Street, Suite 1200,
Wilmington, Delaware 19801
United States

In the rest of the world:
Vernon Press
C/Sancti Espiritu 17,
Malaga, 29006
Spain

Series in Literary Studies

Library of Congress Control Number: 2022939921

ISBN: 978-1-64889-738-2

Also available: 978-1-64889-479-4 [Hardback]; 978-1-64889-614-9 [PDF, E-Book]

Cover design by Vernon Press.

For Beckett, Baxter, and Charley

"Strange. It seems that the most insightful pictures of America are done by Europeans or Blacks [....] I once leafed through a photo book about the West. I was struck by how the Whites figured in the center of the photos and drawings while Blacks were centrifugally distant [....] The blacks were usually, if it were an interior, standing in the doorway. Digging the center."

-Ishmael Reed, *Mumbo Jumbo*

Table of contents

Introduction:
"America is bigger than all of us"

William G. Welty

Rutgers, The State University of New Jersey

Abstract

This introductory essay highlights an (often unspoken) Americanist focus in Post45 studies. It also links this focus to ongoing conversations in World Literature and post-critique. In response, the essay traces a long history in American literature that conceives of "American-ness" as intertwined with global perspectives; that is, one cannot think American literature without world literature, and vice versa. This narrative in turn provides context for the essays contained in the rest of the collection.

Keywords: World Literature, American Literature, Post45, post-critique

***

Much of the work done on the Post45 literary field carries an implicitly Americanist perspective. Even the name of the field suggests a certain literary history, with certain assumptions and blind spots about national spaces, identities, and histories. But what would Post45 look like when considered from outside of the United States? How do the current contours of the field exclude certain voices, both in the United States and elsewhere in the world?[1] And, how would such new perspectives shift the beginning and possible endpoint of that literary period? What new narratives of the contemporary emerge if we begin

---

[1] In a recent issue of *Post45*, Song Hwee Lim poses a similar set of questions about global cinema. He concludes "these sketches reveal the arbitrariness of mapping, always rooted in geopolitics, often shrouded in the myth of the nation, and at once policed and porous. Cinema can both reinforce and question such mappings, not just through the stories it tells on-screen but also via the off-screen activities of making and watching films—often across borders." This collection, then, builds on his work to think of how literature can likewise "reinforce and question such mappings." See Song Hwee Lim, "Toward a Geopolitical Approach to the Study of Transnational Cinema," *Post45 (New Filmic Geographies)*, April 5, 2021, https://post45.org/2021/04/toward-a-geopolitical-approach-to-the-study-of-transnational-cinema/.

telling the story in a different year or from a different national or global perspective? The essays collected in this collection attempt to begin to answer these questions.

Indeed, a story of American literature after 1945 could be told by focusing on the ways texts themselves have created spaces that exist both inside and outside of national spaces. In other words, for contemporary texts, the global might index *both* the outside world, as books circulate within world capitalist markets, and also the "insides" of texts themselves, as the aesthetic features of a text and the experience of reading one can trouble, realign, or even deconstruct national boundaries.[2] To put it in the non-academic terms familiar to any avid bibliophile: reading can transport you to other worlds. Such a critical narrative about contemporary literature would connect the materialist accounts of World Literature scholars like Franco Moretti and Pascale Casanova with the recent resurgence of interest in formalist accounts of texts in Post45 studies.[3] Furthermore, scholars working in the fields of postmodernism and critical race studies have long recognized the inherently international (or, perhaps, trans- or even contra-national) nature of literature in the contemporary. Recently, Amanda Anderson has argued that the so-called "method debates" fail to "capture the energies and commitments of the field, especially given new work on race and ethnicity, queer and trans theory, the environmental humanities, and disability studies."[4] This collection echoes her concern, and attempts to

---

[2] This story draws on Jeffrey Lawrence's account which carefully shows how contemporary American texts defined the non-American as "experience" that could be consumed by the writer from the United States. Conversely, non-American writers imagined the United States as something that could be accessed directly through reading, even if, as was the case for Roberto Bolaño, the writer himself never set foot in the country. See Jeffrey Lawrence, *Anxieties of Experience: The Literatures of the Americas from Whitman to Bolaño* (Oxford: Oxford UP, 2017).

[3] For example, a recent two-part issue of *Post45* was dedicated to formalism. The editors write "But having only recently regained respectability, formalism remains a method whose myriad possible applications have been largely untried. This special issue seeks to illuminate some of its untapped potential. Even with the new interest in questions devoted to understanding 'literariness,' we have yet to explain the difference this new work makes, in part because of the lingering association between formalism and the New Critics [....] What might a true departure from political criticism and its commitment to assessing all cultural forms in ideological terms look like? Might there be other means of asserting the value of form and aesthetic experience? Can form do other kinds of work or make contributions that are distinct from the task of advancing specific ideological aims?" See Timothy Aubry and Florence Dore, "Introduction: Formalism Unbound," *Post45* 5 (2020), https://post45.org/2020/12/aubry-dore-introduction/.

[4] Amanda Anderson, "Situating the Method Debates," *PMLA* 135, no. 5 (October 2020): 1002, https://doi.org/10.1632/pmla.2020.135.5.1002. For an international account

both build on the method debates about and within contemporary literary scholarship while simultaneously placing those debates in a more global context.[5] To echo the language of a recent issue of *Post45*, the essays that follow ask not only "How to be now?" but also "Where to be now?"[6]

Nevertheless, due to both the institutional and ideological makeup of Post45, "contemporary literature" as a field, more often than not, has either rejected these kinds of analyses or worked in separation from them.[7] Perhaps most famously, as attended to by several authors in this collection, Amy Hungerford articulates the critical stance of Post45 in her foundational "On the Period Formerly Known as Contemporary." Hungerford rejects the "cultural materialist accounts" (read: postmodernism) of scholars like Fredric Jameson in favor of a focus on the "specific sociological conditions of the production and consumption of literature" found in work by scholars like Mark McGurl.[8] Put in general terms, she rejects Theory in favor of Historicism.[9] McGurl himself echoes Hungerford in his influential *The Program Era*, writing, "One of the jobs of this book will be to illuminate and appreciate postwar American literature by placing it in this

---

of postmodernism, see François Cusset, *French Theory: How Foucault, Derrida, Deleuze, & Co. Transformed the Intellectual Life of the United States*, trans. Jeff Fort (Minneapolis: University of Minnesota Press, 2008).

[5] Heather Love, herself a foundational figure in the post-critical method debates, recognizes "timeliness" as an essential yet often unachievable quality of scholarship in the contemporary. Due to that often unachievable demand to be timely, emerging as part of the material and existential threats to the university and to literary scholarship, she recognizes that "an expanded sense of the present matters," though she also concludes that the real problem is "raw injustice" rather than any particular methodological debate. Heather Love, "Response," *PMLA* 135, no. 5 (October 2020): 1016, 1019, https://doi.org/10.1632/pmla.2020.135.5.1016.

[6] See, in particular, Sarah Chihaya, Joshua Kotin, and Kinohi Nishikawa, "Introduction: How To Be Now." *Post45* 2 (2019), https://post45.org/2019/07/introduction-how-to-be-now/. In particular, this collection of essays was inspired by Chihaya's, Kotiin's, and Nishikawa's attempt to "invite playful reconfiguration" and an "open-armed, outward-looking orientation [that] creates and recreates conversations that connect the multitudes that define the now now."

[7] There are some notable exceptions to this. See, for example Paul K. Saint-Amour, "Counterfactual States of America: On Parallel Worlds and Longing for the Law," *Post45*, September 20, 2011, https://post45.org/2011/09/counterfactual-states-of-america-on-parallel-worlds-and-longing-for-the-law/.

[8] Amy Hungerford, "On the Period Formerly Known as Contemporary," *American Literary History* 20, no. 1/2 (Spring-Summer 2008): 413, https://doi.org10.1093/alh/ajm044.

[9] The renewed interest in formalist accounts of the contemporary in Post45 suggests that perhaps this rejection was made too hastily.

evolving market context," even if that means that "accounts of individual writers, institutions, and texts must necessarily be, at times, brutally simplified."[10] Since the United States dominates the global market, at least the literary one, it follows then that American literature will dominate the purview of Post45. However, the Post45 commitment to a certain type of scholarship cannot be divorced from the material conditions that generate that scholarship: specifically, its position within prestigious American universities. Hungerford notes that the type of sociological work she upholds as exemplary of Post45 is composed by "a collective of scholars mainly just finishing first books or in the middle of second books" and who were "born at or after the end of the 1960s."[11] Post45, then, is just as much a coterie as a methodology, and a coterie that now exerts significant institutional pressure on the kinds of work on contemporary literature that are seen as valuable.[12]

Other current conversations, loosely grouped under the rubric of "postcritique," also seem to struggle to name the contemporary and articulate how that contemporary relates to the material world around us. Pardis Dabashi insightfully notes, dwelling on the work of postcritical scholars like Rita Felski, Stephen Best, and Sharon Marcus, that "to write about a postcritical future of literary studies and to insufficiently address how grim the future looks to those of us who hold the future of literary studies in our hands seemed a worrisome oversight."[13] Dabashi's critique is twofold: postcritique both misrecognizes the present by focusing on an imagined future that may never arrive, and also fails to address the actual scholars who will someday constitute that future. For her, the issue isn't how we relate to texts themselves, but how we relate to the *world*: "I didn't want to talk differently about texts; I wanted to talk differently about how others were talking about texts."[14] In other words, for the contemporary

---

[10] Mark McGurl, *The Program Era: Postwar Fiction and the Rise of Creative Writing* (Cambridge: Harvard UP, 2009), 15, x.

[11] Hungerford, "On the Period Formerly Known as Contemporary," 416.

[12] The ability of coteries to shape (and sometimes limit) contemporary conversations about literature extends beyond the Post45 group. For example, Stephen Best and Sharon Marcus begin their introduction to the special issue of *Representations* on surface reading by noting that the contributors "constitute a relatively homogenous group of scholars." See Stephen Best and Sharon Marcus, "Surface Reading: An Introduction," *Representations* 108, no. 1 (Fall 2009): 1, https://doi.org/10.1525/rep.2009.108.1.1. Randall Collins suggests that this type of intergenerational influence in fact structures academic discourse in the humanities more generally. See Randall Collins, *The Sociology of Philosophies: A Global Theory of Intellectual Change* (Cambridge: Harvard UP, 1998).

[13] Pardis Dabashi, "Introduction to 'Cultures of Argument': The Loose Garments of Argument," *PMLA* 135, no. 5 (October 2020): 946, https://doi.org/10.1632/pmla.2020.135.5.946.

[14] Dabashi, "Introduction to 'Cultures of Argument,'" 947.

critic, our critical work is not so much about the text itself but the relationships that the text fosters with the other people who make up the world. Thus, a contemporary critique worthy of the name *must* strive after a global perspective, even if such a perspective is also deferred into the "grim future" imagined by Dabashi.

This collection attempts to tell such a story. Specifically, the essays collected here attempt to re-frame the discussions in post45 studies by engaging with non-American writers, texts, and perspectives. Additionally, productive conversations emerge by attempting to think of canonical American writers like Mark Twain and Ishmael Reed from other national and global perspectives. The authors consider both the ways texts themselves as well as their reception histories approach and challenge our understandings of the contemporary. Ultimately, the collection interrogates prevailing narratives of history, culture, identity, and space within the post45 field. In so doing, it re-considers the historical periodization of the field, which currently covers close to 80 years of literary history. While no single collection of essays could ever articulate a truly global perspective, the essays here work towards a new, intertwined narrative about what defines the contemporary and how national and global literatures fit into this moment of world history.

*****

The aim of this collection—to imagine a more global contemporary literary criticism—emerges out of a longstanding concern in American literary texts more generally. Indeed, twentieth-century literary conceptions of America *already* exist as an unstable set of relationships between inside/outside and part/whole. The very linguistic slippage of America for the United States reflects this (I thus use "America," instead of "United States," throughout the introduction to recognize this instability). These "American" texts both invoke spaces *outside* of the nation in order to define America against or from that outsider perspective, and also invoke spaces that are somehow within the nation, but also exist as separate from it. These spatial synecdoches, like the sewer in *Invisible Man*, the amusement park in *Strangers on a Train*, or the movie theater at the end of *Gravity's Rainbow*, bear a unique relationship to the national space while maintaining a feeling of separateness. These extra-national spaces may exist within the space of America or outside of it; they may be represented directly in the text or exist as a sort of "phantom space," only represented in memory or "off-stage." By tracing a history of these spaces across a wide range of writers—from James to Nabokov, from Toomer to Hurston, from Morrison to Coetzee—this introduction indexes the various competing narratives, perspectives, and synecdoches that, through their very incompatibility, reveal America for the disparate collection of spaces, texts, and identities that it is. In so doing, it makes the case that Post45 must be understood within a global context.

Henry James's *The Golden Bowl* both provides an important pivot point between the nineteenth- and twentieth-century novel, and is also a foundational text for thinking about how the twentieth-century novel in America conceives of its relationship to the outside of the nation, as well as to "insides" like subjectivity, memory, and knowledge (our inner mental spaces). National spaces and personal relationships are not only thematically related here—as the Prince's name "Amerigo" suggests—but are both only understandable through the same literary *style*. As James comments on *The Golden Bowl* in the preface to the New York edition, "What perhaps most stands out for me is the still marked inveteracy of *a certain indirect and oblique view* of my present action."[15] While this clearly describes James's style, it also provides a connection between his theory of knowledge and his concept of national space: the space of the Other's consciousness, or of a national imaginary, can only be observed through an "indirect and oblique view." Indeed, America itself is only ever present in the novel in such an indirect and oblique way.

This Jamesian perspective necessarily intermixes concepts of inside and outside. The second volume of the novel "The Princess" begins: "It wasn't till many days had passed that the Princess began to accept the idea of having done, a little, something she was not always doing, or indeed that of having listened to any *inward* voice that spoke in a new tone" (327, emphasis mine). The situation this "inner voice" is commenting on is immediately represented as outer space: "the garden of her life" with "some strange tall tower of ivory, or perhaps rather some wonderfully beautiful but outlandish pagoda" (327). What this inner voice is speaking about is Maggie's desire to enter that Pagoda, whereas before, she had been content to merely walk around it. The pagoda represents Maggie's dawning realization that the mental spaces of others— their secret thoughts, knowledge, desires—not only occupy a prominent position in the "garden of her life," but that the *inside* of such a pagoda is only accessible through a "certain indirect and oblique view." The issue here is not what is hidden on the inside of the pagoda—the knowledge of the Prince's affair with Charlotte—but is instead the existence of such an inaccessible inside to begin with. Here, Maggie's traumatic realization is that other people have their own stories and narratives; indeed, the pagoda scene comes immediately after the first volume of the novel, entitled "The Prince." That volume is the textual

---

[15] Henry James, *The Golden Bowl* (London: Penguin, 2009), 3, emphasis mine. All additional citations will be given in parentheses.

inside of the pagoda, but is inaccessible to Maggie from within her own volume of the novel.

At its most basic level, *The Golden Bowl* stages a confrontation between Europeans like the Prince, who are associated with experience and the knowledge of another's mental space, and Americans like Maggie, who are naïve and *don't know* that others know things that are inaccessible. To put it simply, there seems to be a direct relationship between space/origin and epistemological status: between inner, mental spaces and outer, national ones. Inaccessible spaces, both mental and physical, are intimately connected to the two turning points of the novel. The first is already described above. The second is Maggie's decision to convince her father and Charlotte to return to American City (another inaccessible, phantom place) without Maggie revealing her knowledge of the affair to either of them. Thus, if the pagoda represents the inaccessibility of the Prince's inner space, then American City represents that space for Maggie, since it enables her to maintain her own secret knowledge. Significantly, this phantom space, which is never directly represented in the novel, is paradoxically associated not with an oblique, Jamesian perception but with direct sight. As Maggie and the Prince watch the other couple leave, the Prince says to her, "See? I see nothing but *you*" (595, emphasis in original). The novel moves from thoughts of London in its opening pages to thoughts of American City on its final page, and likewise moves from "indirect and oblique" perception to direct perception. But this direct perception is one that involves not seeing as well as seeing. It encompasses the unrepresented space of American City and the present spaces of England, through a form of sight that is doubly qualified, first as a question—"See?"—and second as perception that must first see "nothing" before it can reach its desired object. American City thus enables the kind of perception necessary for "seeing" the space of America itself: perception that both sees and doesn't see; that moves between shifting borders of inside and outside, known and unknown.

Moving forward into the postwar period, Vladimir Nabokov's *Lolita* likewise interrogates the relationship between outside and inside and between Europe and the United States.[16] Furthermore, Nabokov also suggests there is an intimate connection between knowing (epistemological, perceptual, and sexual) and national space. But compared to James, the one-to-one associations of space and theme are less clear. After James re-frames what perception and knowledge

---

[16] McGurl begins his introduction to *The Program Era* by reading *Lolita* in terms of Nabokov's position within the American Academy, where the "powerful fantasy" is not so much Humbert's "pathologically narcissistic love for Lolita," but rather "one of ideal working conditions, a release from the prison of the classroom into the richly reflexive freedom of artistic expression." See McGurl, *The Program Era*, 2.

are at the end of *The Golden Bowl* and locates that shift to a specifically American space, *Lolita* picks up those ideas and plays out their implications in that American national space.[17] While *The Golden Bowl* represents a confrontation between American naiveté and European knowledge, *Lolita* depicts the aftermath of the deconstruction of those binaries, where knowledge and innocence, European-ness and American-ness, inside and outside all exist as an unstable system within the national space of the United States. As Humbert and Lolita are concluding their first cross-country roadtrip, Humbert reflects:

> We had been everywhere. We had really seen nothing. And I catch myself thinking today that our long journey had only *defiled* with a sinuous trail of slime the lovely, trustful, dreamy, enormous country that by then, in retrospect, *was no more to us than a collection* of dog-eared maps, ruined tour books, old tires, and her sobs in the night—every night, every night—the moment I feigned sleep.[18]

Like James, Nabokov here intermixes topography and perception, so that "being" and "seeing" are related but not completely compatible states. Additionally, Humbert's "We had really seen *nothing*" echoes the Prince's "See? I see *nothing* but you," so that, in both cases, a form of indirect perception is demanded by a particular national space. This sight, in turn, results in "defilement," a breakdown of the clean barriers between inside and outside, innocence and experience, knowledge and ignorance. After such a defilement, both subjectivity and nationality no longer seem whole and can only be represented metaphorically as collections of parts. Damaged representations of space ("dog-eared maps, ruined tour books") substitute for an understanding of the national space itself. And instead of the precise language of James, the metaphorical substitutes for Lolita's interiority are her wordless sobs.

Like *The Golden Bowl* and *Lolita*, Jean Toomer's *Cane* also wrestles with how perception frames national identity and space, but Toomer also explicitly tracks how race affects the ways subjects inhabit spaces and perspectives. *Cane* portrays the United States as a collection of disparate parts and places (not only

---

[17] The difference in Nabokov's treatment of America compared to James's can partially be accounted for by the former's feelings about the latter. In a letter to Edmund Wilson, Nabokov refers to a book by James as "miserable stuff, a complete fake" and suggests "you ought to debunk that pale porpoise and his plush vulgarities some day." See Emily Temple, "The Meanest Things Vladimir Nabokov Said About Other Writers," *Literary Hub*, April 20, 2018, https://lithub.com/the-meanest-things-vladimir-nabokov-said-about-other-writers/.

[18] Vladimir Nabokov, *Lolita* (New York: Vintage, 1997), 175-176, my emphases. Additional citations in parentheses.

in terms of space, but also in terms of textuality) by blurring the lines between a novel and a *collection* of stories or poems. *Cane* is animated by movement between different spaces, from the American South to the American North, and back again. But unlike the other two texts, where the protagonists are free to move about at will, *Cane* instead questions which subjects are able to inhabit which spaces, specifically with regard to race and gender. The first division in the text, between South and North, is marked by a half circle, and the second division between North and South by an incomplete semi-circle. Thus, as the text moves between different regions, it also seems to approach completion without achieving it, or to move full circle without ever quite finishing its circuit. The third section, occupied entirely by the "Kabnis" story, depicts the conflict resulting from the inability of certain racialized subjects to inhabit certain regional spaces: specifically, the problems faced by the Black Northerner Kabnis living in a small Southern town. Kabnis's inability to fully take part in the life of his Southern town dramatizes the text's refusal to "complete the circle," to return to its beginnings in the South and inhabit that space. That is, there is a misfit between subject and space, symbolized by the gaps in the circles that separate the different sections of the book. There is also a misfit between subjects and texts. "Kabnis" begins with the titular character's inability to read, and concludes with another failure of text: "th sin th white folks 'mitted when they made th Bible lie."[19] Like *Lolita*, which suggests an affinity between damaged texts (maps and tourbooks), space, and subjectivity, *Cane* demonstrates the failure of space to under-*write* identity. In so doing, *Cane* shows that within the collection of parts that make up the nation, there is also the "part of no part," to borrow a phrase from Jacques Rancière.[20] An affinity with a certain national space might enable certain kinds of subjectivity and perception, but at the cost of stifling others. Indeed, "Kabnis" recognizes relationships between space and subjectivity, but frames them as oppressive. For example, "Through Ramsay, the whole white South weighs down upon him. The pressure is terrific" (100). Here, Ramsay symbolically stands in for the entire South, not as a legible text, but as a crushing weight.

While recognizing these difficulties, *Cane* still attempts a similar gesture as those found in James and Nabokov: to re-define the relationship between subject, space, and perception. If the incomplete circles that divide the text don't return to their origin and complete their circuit, this allows for a different conclusion, rather than a repetition of the same oppressive history. Instead of a return to the same, the incomplete circle generates new (re)productive

---

[19] Jean Toomer, *Cane* (New York: Liveright, 1993), 115. All additional citations in parentheses.
[20] See Jacques Rancière, *Dissensus: On Politics and Aesthetics*, trans. Steven Corcoran (London: Continuum, 2010).

possibilities. Indeed, "Kabnis" ends with repeated imagery of new birth juxtaposed with an intermingling of inside and outside: "*Within its soft circle*, the figures of Carrie and Father John. *Outside*, the sun arises from its cradle" (116, emphases mine). The incomplete circle that separates this story from section two reappears here, but, instead of signaling failure, it frames a new couple. And its very incompleteness is what allows for new birth, suggesting a transition from the couple on the inside to the sun on the outside, which sings a "birth-song slanting down gray dust streets and sleepy windows of the southern town" (116). The last two words of the text gesture both at a specific place and at the larger region of the South as a unit of national space. Rather than signalling an absent extra-national space, this text concludes by aligning a present space with rebirth, though an ambivalent one.

Toomer and other writers of color like Hurston, Baldwin, Wright, Himes, and Ellison, present a counter-narrative to that of James and Nabokov, expressing both desire for and anxiety about the American "melting pot" narrative.[21] For example, *Invisible Man* returns full circle at the end to the underground space from where it began, repeating *Cane's* desire to imagine the subject from outside to inside, while also inverting the text's final movement from inside to outside. Also like *Cane*, *Invisible Man* concludes by uneasily dwelling on the possibility of the country as a disparate collection or collectivity, so that the "lower frequencies" where "I speak for you" represent both a collective voice and the eclipse of certain voices by others.[22] In an analogous way to Toomer's re-imagining of inside/outside, Ishmael Reed's *Mumbo Jumbo* re-imagines the extra-national, bringing together a skepticism of the melting pot narrative and a combination of perspectives from both inter-, intra-, and extra-national spaces in order to compose a portrait of America.

Reed turns to extra-national spaces in order to account for alternative histories that are obscured by a limited national or spatial perspective. Instead of imagining from the outside to the inside, Reed imagines the outside *into* the inside by tracing the spread of "Jes' Grew" across America. "Jes' Grew," a global pandemic associated with joy and dancing, also brings with it a text of alternative history, "The Work," that originates in Egypt and circulates the globe before finally making its way to America. Through the movements of "Jes' Grew," America itself becomes extra-national, able to contain real history and the alternative history of The Work within the intermixed spaces of Egypt, the

---

[21] For an early critique of other pastoral imaginaries about American culture, see Leo Marx, *The Machine in the Garden: Technology and the Pastoral Ideal in America* (Oxford: Oxford UP, 1964). Marx, however, is largely silent on issues of race.

[22] Ralph Ellison, *Invisible Man* (New York: Vintage, 1995), 581. Additional citations in parentheses.

US, and Haiti. In the epilogue to the novel, Reed's protagonist reflects on the type of perception necessary to portray such an odd, extra-national space:

> Strange. It seems that the most insightful pictures of America are done by Europeans or Blacks [....] I once leafed through a photo book about the West. I was struck by how the Whites figured in the center of the photos and drawings while Blacks were centrifugally distant [....] The blacks were usually, if it were an interior, standing in the doorway. Digging the center.[23]

This is not an essentialist claim about non-Americans knowing America better, or a banal claim about the truer sight of the outsider's gaze. If that were true, there would be no significant difference between the perspective of the writers the narrator names—"Wright, Baldwin, Himes"—and the "outsider" émigré writers who were "actually" American—Hemingway, Miller, and so on. Instead, this is a structural claim, suggesting that historically "Europeans or Blacks" were able to (or forced to) occupy a position allowing them to "[dig] the center" without claiming that gaze is inherent to that type of subject. Indeed, the "picture" painted by Reed here is empty of content, instead only concerned with deixis: "West," "center," "distant," "interior," "doorway," "center." With this in mind, the "most insightful picture" of America becomes a *picture without content*, a pure image or a pure phantom space. But at the same time, such a structure can accommodate any content, and does so in Reed's novel: America can include Reed's pastiche of multiple genres and styles, Haiti and Egypt, the texts of history cited at the end alongside the alternative history of The Work, and photo and text.

With the US reframed as a picture without content, contemporary writers *turn back to history* with a strong desire to describe the real and account for the subjects who have been the victims of reframing, excluded from the picture of American-ness altogether: Sebald's photographs in *The Emigrants*, Morrison's "60 million and more" that begins *Beloved*, or Bolaño's forensic accounting of violence against women in *2666*, to name just a few prominent examples. In J. M. Coetzee's *Dusklands*, Eugene Dawn, a researcher working on something called "The Vietnam Project," reflects specifically on how America gets imagined: "This is because she [his wife] has a false conception of America. She cannot believe that America is big enough to contain its deviants. But America is bigger than all of us [...] America will swallow me, digest me, dissolve me in the tides of its blood."[24] Like Reed's expansive portrait of America, Coetzee's novel can structurally accommodate various world spaces within the text,

---

[23] Ishmael Reed, *Mumbo Jumbo* (New York: Scribner, 1996), 209-210.
[24] J. M. Coetzee, *Dusklands* (New York: Penguin, 1982), 9.

specifically Vietnam, America, and South Africa. At the same time, in response to this structure that can accommodate any content, Coetzee turns to history to take account of real trauma and violence; indeed, the two narratives of the text demonstrate that it is the same structural violence at the foundation of imperialism in South Africa and in the US involvement in Vietnam. Thus, Coetzee shows how the structural emptiness of America can become an imperialist gesture, so that the entire world is subsumed by the United States, but he also shows how that desire turns against itself, inwards, so that becoming "American" means getting swallowed up and digested. Both Reed and Coetzee invoke history to account for the violence produced by a concept of America as an unstable and shifting collection of insides and outsides. These writers also show how the picture of America can accommodate new kinds of writing and authorial subjects. And this desire to account for history in turn places a demand on literary criticism: to continue to understand the shifting spaces of inside and outside, and to work towards understanding not only the novel in America, but the American novel in the world.

*****

The collection is divided into three parts. Part I, entitled "How Soon Is Now?" dwells on the temporal nature of Post45. The authors debate whether the contemporary has any definiable qualities as a historical moment, or whether the contemporary is simply whatever moment we happen to find ourselves in. Amanda Lagji's essay develops the former position through a reading of Ishtiyaq Shukri's *The Silent Minaret,* whereas Michael Maguire-Khan develops the latter position through an engagement with the work of Adorno and others. Dan Malinowski likewise attempts to develop a sense of the specific qualities of the contemporary, but does so through a critique of the Post45 group and a return to the work of Marx and Hegel. Each essay attempts to answer the question: is the contemporary always just "now"? And if not, when is it?

Part II tackles the spatial aspect of post45 Studies. The authors build on the debates of Part I in order to strive towards more global perspectives on texts from the Soviet Union, Nigeria, the Dominican Republic, and the United States. Daria Goncharova focuses on a Soviet-era film adaptation of *The Adventures of Huckleberry Finn,* tracing how the film reimagines its source material to focus on an anti-capitalist critique of the United States and its treatment of African Americans. Cathryn Piwinski focuses on the various paratexts of *The Brief Wondrous Life of Oscar Wao* by Junot Díaz in order to suggest that the novel itself mounts a potential critique of globalized literary culture. And Pritika Pradhan reads Chimamanda Ngozi Adichie's *Americanah* as reimagining the contemporary global migrant narrative, but then struggling to live up to the premise of its own reimaginings.

Of course, a short collection of essays can never truly capture a global perspective, and the final section of this collection wrestles with that very problem. In chapter seven, Sushil Sivaram discusses Indian literature and attempts to work out what sort of *practice* might best situate us as literary scholars to inhabit the world and the contemporary, whatever their complicated relationship is. In other words, to borrow his own language, he dwells on what it might mean to take post45 itself as an object of study. The collection ends with a brief coda which locates these debates and lines of inquiry in the post-Trumpian moment of the United States.

The essays collected here thus emerge out of a long and ongoing, yet often unremarked upon, conversation within literary texts themselves. However, these essays also emerge out of a very specific set of contemporary social and political conversations: conversations that mirror the relationship between the novel in America and contemporary global literature more generally. Many of the pieces collected here began with a panel at the 2019 NeMLA Conference, appropriately held in Washington D. C. That same weekend, Robert Mueller had concluded his report on Donald Trump's potential collusion with Russia in the 2016 election and William Barr had released his summary of the review. Washington D. C. was abuzz with talk about the report, and indeed, that political conversation mirrored and refracted our literary conversations throughout the whole weekend. On the one hand, the Mueller report emphasized the United States' connection to the world at large, and specifically to Russia. On the other, it also recognized that those connections were often obscure and hard to parse, though the report was also extremely clear that it did *not* exonerate Trump. In the years since that conference, Trump's actions, particularly regarding the COVID pandemic, continued that trend; the Trump presidency and its aftermath has simultaneously de-centered, re-emphasized, and deconstructed the relationship of the United States to the rest of the world. Thus, the essays in this collection speak to that ongoing and urgent political conversation: about the place of the United States in the World, and the fraught and shifting nature of that relationship.

Works cited

Anderson, Amanda. "Situating the Method Debates." *PMLA* 135, no. 5 (October 2020): 1002-1008. https://doi.org/10.1632/pmla.2020.135.5.1002.

Aubry, Timothy, and Florence Dore. "Introduction: Formalism Unbound." *Post45* 5 (2020). https://post45.org/2020/12/aubry-dore-introduction/.

Best, Stephen, and Sharon Marcus. "Surface Reading: An Introduction." *Representations* 108, no. 1 (Fall 2009): 1-21. https://doi.org/10.1525/rep.2009.108.1.1.

Chihaya, Sarah, Joshua Kotin, and Kinohi Nishikawa. "Introduction: How To Be Now." *Post45* 2 (2019). https://post45.org/2019/07/introduction-how-to-be-now.

Coetzee, J. M. *Dusklands*. New York: Penguin, 1982.

Collins, Randall. *The Sociology of Philosophies: A Global Theory of Intellectual Change*. Cambridge: Harvard UP, 1998.

Cusset, François. *French Theory: How Foucault, Derrida, Deleuze, & Co. Transformed the Intellectual Life of the United States*. Translated by Jeff Fort. Minneapolis: University of Minnesota Press, 2008.

Dabashi, Pardis. "Introduction to 'Cultures of Argument': The Loose Garments of Argument." *PMLA* 135, no. 5 (October 2020): 946-955. https://doi.org/10.1632/pmla.2020.135.5.946.

Ellison, Ralph. *Invisible Man*. New York: Vintage, 1995.

Hungerford, Amy. "On the Period Formerly Known as Contemporary." *American Literary History* 20, no. 1/2 (Spring-Summer 2008): 410-419. https://doi.org/10.1093/alh/ajm044.

James, Henry. *The Golden Bowl*. London: Penguin, 2009.

Lawrence, Jeffrey. *Anxieties of Experience: The Literatures of the Americas from Whitman to Bolaño*. Oxford: Oxford UP, 2017.

Lim, Song Hwee. "Toward a Geopolitical Approach to the Study of Transnational Cinema." *Post45 (New Filmic Geographies)*, April 5, 2021. https://post45.org/2021/04/toward-a-geopolitical-approach-to-the-study-of-transnational-cinema/.

Love, Heather. "Response." *PMLA* 135, no. 5 (October 2020): 1016-1020. https://doi.org/10.1632/pmla.2020.135.5.1016.

Marx, Leo. *The Machine in the Garden: Technology and the Pastoral Ideal in America*. Oxford: Oxford UP, 1964.

McGurl, Mark. *The Program Era: Postwar Fiction and the Rise of Creative Writing*. Cambridge: Harvard UP, 2009.

Nabokov, Vladimir. *Lolita*. New York: Vintage, 1997.

Rancière, Jacques. *Dissensus: On Politics and Aesthetics*. Translated by Steven Corcoran. London: Continuum, 2010.

Reed, Ishmael. *Mumbo Jumbo*. New York: Scribner, 1996.

Saint-Amour, Paul K. "Counterfactual States of America: On Parallel Worlds and Longing for the Law." *Post45*, September 20, 2011. https://post45.org/2011/09/counterfactual-states-of-america-on-parallel-worlds-and-longing-for-the-law/.

Temple, Emily. "The Meanest Things Vladimir Nabokov Said About Other Writers." *Literary Hub*, April 20, 2018. https://lithub.com/the-meanest-things-vladimir-nabokov-said-about-other-writers/.

Toomer, Jean. *Cane*. New York: Liveright, 1993.

Section I.
"How Soon Is Now?"

Chapter 1

Contemporaneity is a chronological, not a qualitative category

Michael Maguire-Khan

Penn State University

Abstract

This essay argues against recent attempts to invest "the contemporary" with qualitative content, arguing instead for a purely chronological, deictic definition of contemporary literature. First, I articulate certain impasses in the study of contemporary literature as a result of its prior identifications with historical, chronological, and aesthetic periods (post-World War II, twentieth-century, postmodernism). Second, I demonstrate that any qualitative definition of contemporary literature will necessarily periodize the field and unnecessarily narrow its focus. Finally, I propose a chronological understanding of contemporary literature as a means of leveraging those aspects of contemporary literature that complicate or do not conform with the methodological norms of earlier periods.

Keywords: Contemporary Literature, Chronology, Aesthetics, Historicism

***

Although something by the name of "contemporary literature" has been taught and studied in the American university for over sixty years, there exists no commonly accepted theory, history, or even definition of the field as an institutional discipline or object of scholarship. Nor, still, has there been any sustained effort to produce such a theory, history, or definition; indeed, it is only within the last few years that a handful of scholars have begun such work. This lack of disciplinary self-consciousness has become a particularly significant problem in recent decades. Literary scholarship has since the 1980s favored historicist modes of reading that, in practice, place a premium on what is regarded as sufficient chronological distance between the researcher and the object of study; in other words, the dominant mode of literary scholarship presupposes non-contemporaneity. There are several reasons for this partiality to chronological distance, many of which were long used to justify the exclusion of contemporary literature from university study. In the case of the scholarship dominant today, this distance is crucial to certain forms of historicism in which the scholar, usually drawing on historical research from other fields (history, sociology, economics, etc.), retrospectively articulates a cultural matrix in which literary text and social context determine and overdetermine each other.

Of course, contemporary works can still be (and are) attached to an ongoing metanarrative, such as that of the neoliberal stage of capital or the historical "rupture" represented by 9/11, but the historical proximity mitigates the authority of both the metanarrative and the literary object. As a consequence of literary scholarship's structural predisposition to historical distance, contemporary literature studies, which constitutively lacks a fixed chronological scope (let alone a stable "period" as its object) stands at a methodological disadvantage relative to period-fields like nineteenth-century literature studies and modernist studies, at least insofar as it remains beholden to normative methodological and professional practices. The failure of contemporary literature studies to recognize its difference, or at least fully articulate the implications of this difference, is the principal impetus for this essay.

In addition to the underlying problems the field of contemporary literature studies has struggled to resolve since the rise of historicism in the 1980s, the turn of the twenty-first century entailed a more immediately visible crisis within the field. Between the felt and actual decline of postmodernism as a periodizing concept (that is, as a historical concept organizing literary production since the late 1960s) and the necessary dis-identification of "late twentieth-century literature" with "contemporary literature" after 2000, scholars were forced to inquire about the relationship between such terms as "postwar literature," "late-twentieth-century literature," "postmodern literature," "twenty-first-century literature," and "contemporary literature."[1] Another way to put this is that scholars were compelled to recognize that "contemporary literature" is not a period-field in the same way that "nineteenth-century literature" is. "Contemporary" is a deictic term, necessarily dependent on the scholar's temporal circumstances; thus, the object of contemporary literature studies is always mutable, always on the move.

---

[1] See, for instance, two twenty-first-century special issues of *Twentieth-Century Literature*—a journal whose eponymous object was at the point of its founding only half-complete, but is now cut off from the present: *After Postmodernism* 53, no. 3 (Fall 2007) and *Postmodernism, Then* 57, no. 3/4 (Fall/Winter 2011).

In the last 15 or so years, contemporary literature studies has made important strides toward recognizing, theorizing, and promoting itself as a distinctive field. In 2006, a group of junior scholars formed Post45, a collective that has since founded an annual conference and, in 2010, an online peer-reviewed journal of the same name. Around the same time, a separate group of scholars began to form the Association for the Study of the Arts of the Present (ASAP), which has hosted its own conferences and symposia since 2009 and introduced *ASAP/Journal* in 2016. Additionally, a number of presses have launched book series in recent years dedicated to the study of contemporary literature broadly understood: Stanford University Press' *Post45* (edited by the titular collective), Columbia University Press' *Literature Now*, and the University of Iowa Press' *The New American Canon*.[2]

With such institution building has come increased scholarly attention to contemporary literature studies as a distinct discipline. The last few years have featured a number of edited collections—in addition to this one—which, to varying degrees, interrogate the composition and meaning of contemporary literature as a field of study. The collection *Postmodern/Postwar—And After* (2016), for instance, contains a compelling "dialogue on the field" in which a number of scholars mull recent developments in the discipline. Concerning the rise of post-1945 literature's institutional visibility, Matthew Hart posits three possible causes: 1) the passing of time, which makes possible "new sorts of scholarship, whether historicist or not" and "the sort of work that gets recognized and rewarded by our colleagues, most of whom assume such focal distance as a matter of course;" 2) market pressures, which make the popularity of contemporary texts with students more valuable; and, 3) the rise of modernist studies, which has "given us institutional structures to imitate and react against."[3] Speaking as editor of *The New American Canon* series, Samuel Cohen worries that the "accelerated expansion" of the field has reinforced an "inclination so many of us share to obsess about periodization, movements, and moments," and that the desires "to have a new name for everything, to build schema in which the difference of now from then can be charted . . . can also breed a predictability and, perhaps, more important, can restrict the ways

---

[2] For recent commentaries on the field's institutional growth, see David J. Alworth, "Hip to Post45," *Contemporary Literature* 54, no. 3 (Fall 2013): 622-633, https://www.jstor.org/stable/43297925; and Theodore Martin, "Contemporary Inc.," *Representations* 142 (Spring 2018): 124-144, https://doi.org/10.1525/rep.2018.142.1.124.

[3] Andrew Hoberek et al., "Postmodern, Postwar, Contemporary: A Dialogue on the Field," in *Postmodern/Postwar—and After: Rethinking American Literature*, ed. Jason Gladstone, Andrew Hoberek, and Daniel Worden (Iowa City: University of Iowa Press, 2016), 29.

we think and talk about aesthetic and social history."[4] Connecting Hart's and Cohen's insights, we can observe that the kind of scholarship the organization of contemporary literature studies as "post-1945" enables and encourages is precisely the preoccupation with attaining enough distance from the present to name and periodize it in emulation of the historical scholarship that dominates twentieth-century (and earlier) literary studies. **"Post-1945" facilitates a stable disciplinary identity by domesticating the challenging alterity of contemporary literature as an object of study.**

"The contemporary" itself has of late become a potent site of discourse across several disciplinary fields, especially philosophy and art history, calling attention to a term that has remained largely untheorized even as "modernity" and its cognates have been endlessly dissected. Perhaps the most extensive study of the meaning of the term "contemporary" in "contemporary literature" to date, Theodore Martin's *Contemporary Drift: Genre, Historicism, and the Problem of the Present* offers a compelling argument for the usefulness of literary genres to historicizing the present and to determine "what is contemporary and what is not."[5] Among a number of "theses on the concept of the contemporary" with which Martin introduces his book, especially pertinent is his argument that "the contemporary is not a period," for it is "an unreliable form of historical measure, a periodizing term that doesn't quite manage to periodize. With no agreed-on beginning and no ending in sight, the contemporary does not so much delimit history as drift across it."[6] While I am largely in agreement here, contemporary literature was initially assimilated into the curriculum as if it *were* a period-field like any other. One consequence of treating contemporary literature as a period-field has been that the critical methodologies, presuppositions, and scholarly conventions developed in other period-fields have been brought to bear on contemporary literature without heed of its essential difference. Martin's project is immensely useful for thinking about "how the formal conventions of contemporary artworks allow us to envision the historical coherence of the contemporary world" in order to "learn to practice historicism by other means."[7] What I want to argue here, rather differently, is that there is much to be gained by seeking *not only* to integrate contemporary literature into the institutional norms of historicism and periodization—processes that will ineluctably happen in due time—but

---

[4] Hoberek et al., "Postmodern, Postwar, Contemporary," 35.

[5] Theodore Martin, *Contemporary Drift: Genre, Historicism, and the Problem of the Present* (New York: Columbia UP, 2017), 7.

[6] Martin, *Contemporary Drift*, 2.

[7] Martin, *Contemporary Drift*, 197.

also by exploring and harnessing the ways in which contemporary literature resists those same disciplinary conventions.

As one example of such a project, Amy Hungerford's *Making Literature Now* interrogates the distinctive challenges and affordances of studying what she felicitously calls a "present-tense archive." Noting that "Scholarly conversations . . . continue to coalesce around a small group of figures" within the English department, Hungerford observes with some skepticism that "scholars thinking about the second half of the 20ᵗʰ century and the start of the 21ˢᵗ are, it seems, busy trying to accomplish a similarly narrow selection to serve that later period. Building a canon of more recent work allows us to talk about books we have read in common—always a pleasure—and helps scholars to publish, and thus to move along in their careers."[8] The methodology of Hungerford's book is an eclectic mix of sociology of reading, scholarly reporting, and close reading. What is most unique is her willingness to take advantage, through interview and observation, of the fact that its subjects are still living and to "swim against the canonical tide" by engaging the "crowd of writers who no longer write, or of writers who are culturally invisible" as a means of preserving "a recent past that doesn't qualify as history and yet has already been dismissed from our urgent present."[9]

Such institutional duress not only fuels the race to canonize and periodize the literary production of the present, but reinforces the privileging of the recent past or formerly contemporary over that urgent present. This tendency is most clearly represented in the displacement of contemporary literature by "post-1945" literature. The formation of Post45 constitutes the most visible and influential institutionalization of contemporary literature studies, and yet its emphasis on 1945 threatens to subordinate the study of the present and its unique challenges to a historicization of the second half of the twentieth century on the same normative model as nineteenth-century and modernist scholarship. Mary Esteve, one of Post45's founding members, describes the collective's original aims thus:

> When the research collective Post45 formed in 2006, it was less interested, I think, in challenging the historiography of periodization than in asserting the validity of historicizing (or contextualizing) the literature and culture of a recognizable period dominated by too few methodological paradigms (primarily the ones Andy [Hoberek] and Amy [Elias] cite: postmodernism, poststructuralism, author studies, ethnic studies, etc.). Some of Post45's founders have roots in areas of scholarship where

---

[8] Amy Hungerford, *Making Literature Now* (Stanford: Stanford UP, 2016), 15-16.

[9] Hungerford, *Making Literature Now,* 16, 17.

historicist methodologies have become the norm—pre-1945 modernism and late nineteenth-century American studies—and no doubt an element of frontierism factored into their commitment to developing alternative approaches to post-1945 literature and culture.[10]

The problem here is not so much the historicist approaches to late twentieth-century literature themselves but rather that framing contemporary literature as "post-1945" effectively marginalizes the contemporaneity of contemporary literature and its challenge to periodization in favor of objects that can be more easily historicized and periodized.[11]

Ironically, the closest approximation to a "post-1945" manifesto is Amy Hungerford's "On the Period Formerly Known as the Contemporary" (2008). Then at work on *Postmodern Belief,* a study of post-1960 American literature, Hungerford wrote that there is "even at Post45, some evinced discomfort at writing about the literature of the late [twentieth] century even if we do now teach it with greater confidence, suggesting once again that focal distance may finally be necessary in order to see the past clearly, something historians have long known."[12] In the end, Hungerford suggests that we simply use the term "contemporary" to designate "the period that began somewhere around the middle of the twentieth century and which we still, probably, inhabit."[13] Such a chronologically extensive "contemporary"—certainly not, taking the word's etymology seriously, "together in time" with me or the scholars around Hungerford's age who formed Post45—effectively collapses the distinction between the actual, felt present and a past that can be confidently historicized. I consider the shift in her thinking represented by *Making Literature Now* a salutary, if not representative, one, though as she herself notes with respect to her earlier essay, "The historicism of the field now seems like a question and not a given."[14] This essay participates in that questioning.

As has been shown, the meaning of the "contemporary" in contemporary literature and art, long taken for granted as a term that designates a vague

---

[10] Hoberek et al., "Postmodern, Postwar, Contemporary," 36.

[11] Throughout the dialogue on the field quoted above, "Post45" and "contemporary" literature studies are frequently used interchangeably. My point here is certainly not that one must choose to study either one or the other, but that "Post45" encompasses contemporary literature, obscuring the difference between studying the 1950s and studying the 2010s in 2022.

[12] Amy Hungerford, "On the Period Formerly Known as Contemporary," *American Literary History* 20, no. 1/2 (Spring-Summer 2008): 418, https://doi.org/10.1093/alh/ajm044.

[13] Hungerford, "On the Period Formerly Known as Contemporary," 418.

[14] Hungerford, *Making Literature Now,* 186.

present defined primarily in contrast to a once-synonymous, but now un-contemporary "modern," has in the last few years become the subject of fervent debate. The widespread perception that the "postmodern," variously defined, is no longer an adequate descriptor of present culture has led many to turn toward "contemporary," a term that both predated and survived its identification with postmodernism, as a kind of natural successor to the modern. [15] The original sense of "modern" was mainly indexical and empty of qualitative content—"Its earliest English senses were nearer our contemporary, in the sense of something existing now, just now"—but prior to the Renaissance it assumed epochal definition in contrast with "ancient" and, by the late nineteenth and twentieth centuries, was assigned positive qualitative content in the arts, especially in the form of "modernism." [16] A similar, though more deliberate, phenomenon is at work in the attempt to redefine "contemporary" as a qualitative category, possessing positive features à la modernism or postmodernism, and to discard its more comprehensive, quotidian signification of "belonging to or occurring in the present." Michael North has perceptively observed that, "though the modern has been severed from the present, ideas about the present are still strongly conditioned by the modern. All the terms for *now*, including *contemporary*, seem to have lost their deictic function, their purely relative significance, and are expected to have a particular quality, on the model of the modern." [17] Thus, not only have a number of scholars put forward periodizations of contemporary literature building on a former modernism (digimodernism, post-postmodernism, cosmodernism, etc.), but still, others have identified "the contemporary" as a signifier for our present possessing particular qualitative content. [18] The point I want to stress is that such attempts to define "contemporary" qualitatively—to detach it from its

---

[15] For arguments in favor of "the contemporary" as a periodization of the present, see Terry Smith, "Contemporary Art and Contemporaneity," *Critical Inquiry* 32, no. 4 (Summer 2006): 681-707, https://doi.org/10.1086/508087; and Peter Osborne, *Anywhere or Not at All: Philosophy of Contemporary Art* (New York: Verso, 2013).

[16] Raymond Williams, *Keywords: A Vocabulary of Culture and Society* (Oxford: Oxford UP, 2015), 155.

[17] Michael North, *What Is the Present?* (Princeton: Princeton UP, 2018), 83.

[18] On digimodernism see Alan Kirby, *Digimodernism: How New Technologies Dismantle the Postmodern and Reconfigure Our Culture* (New York: Continuum, 2009). On post-postmodernism, see Jeffrey T. Nealon, *Post-Postmodernism; Or, the Cultural Logic of Just-in-Time Capitalism* (Stanford: Stanford UP, 2012). On cosmodernism, see Christian Moraru, *Cosmodernism: American Narrative, Late Globalization, and the New Cultural Imaginary* (Ann Arbor: University of Michigan Press, 2011). For a helpful survey of these various designations, see Emily Hyde and Sarah Wasserman, "The Contemporary," *Literature Compass* 14, no. 9 (September 2017): 1-19, https://doi.org/10.1111/lic3.12411.

deictic signification and, in the process, suggest that any element existing in the present can be *more or less* contemporary—necessarily adhere to a historicist logic ill-suited to the study of contemporary literature. Such epochal definitions effectively reify the present, prematurely commencing the historiographic reflexes of canonization and periodization. Instead, I propose that contemporary literature studies embrace a banally empty, chronological definition of "contemporary" as a means of maintaining the field's fundamental openness to the heterogeneity and possibility of the present.[19] The purpose of advocating for chronology rather than periodization, for description prior to demarcation, is founded on the belief that many of our normative approaches to historicizing the past are inadequate to an understanding of the present. The limitations of these approaches, which share a denial of coevalness and an assertion of teleology in their aesthetic nonsynchronism, are elaborated on in the following section.

Aesthetic nonsychronism and its discontents

In *Minima Moralia*, Theodor Adorno recalls a music teacher who attempted to dissuade him of his preference for the atonal music of Schoenberg. Believing Adorno's interest lay in the wish to be aesthetically fashionable, the instructor contended that "the ultra-modern . . . was no longer modern," and in fact had been superseded by neo-classicism.[20] Though it pains him, Adorno admits the truth of the teacher's assessment. What Adorno had recognized as modern—a formally disruptive avant-gardism, based on the most advanced artistic material—is no longer dominant: "The modern has really become unmodern. Modernity is a qualitative, not a chronological, category."[21] The political significance of this distinction can be grasped with reference to Ernst Bloch's

---

[19] This proposal has considerable affinity with that of the editors of the special issue of *Post45*, "How to Be Now." In their introduction, the editors endorse critical pluralism and deemphasize periodization as fruitful responses to contemporary cultural production. This special issue notably grew out of a conference titled "The Contemporary" and, though there are traces of quasi-periodization in the introduction's early reference to a capital-c contemporary, the editors' substitution of "now" as their key term seems instructive and, I think, productive. See Sarah Chihaya, Joshua Kotin, and Kinohi Nishikawa, "Introduction: How to Be Now," *Post45* 2 (2019), https://post45.org/2019/07/introduction-how-to-be-now.

[20] In what might serve as a further case against Frankfurt-tinged nonsynchronous periodizations of the present, Fredric Jameson reproduced what Adorno took to be the regrettably dominant aesthetic mode of the early twentieth century (neo-classicism) as the regrettably dominant aesthetic mode of the *late* twentieth century (pastiche).

[21] Theodor W. Adorno, *Minima Moralia: Reflections on a Damaged Life*, trans. E. F. N. Jephcott (New York: Verso, 2005), 218.

earlier theorization of "nonsynchronism." In a 1935 essay, Bloch declared that "not all people exist in the same Now. They do so only externally, by virtue of the fact that they may all be seen today. But that does not mean that they are living at the same time with others."[22] Bloch was of course referring to the rise of Nazism, which he understood as a collective retreat to the past against the "unbearable Now" of capitalism, rather than neo-classicism. But Adorno came to view nonsynchronism within the arts as a symptom of political regression. Thus the modern was, for Adorno, an essentially transhistorical ideal that only temporarily assumed the status of the dominant or norm, and any art not committed to the most advanced forms was *a priori* politically reactionary.[23] In the abstract, nonsynchronous conceptions of the present are not inherently progressive or conservative. On the one hand, nonsynchronism can be thought in the form of a multiplicity of co-present temporalities against a single hegemonic historical narrative, resulting in a "heterogeneous coevality."[24] For Bloch, Adorno, and the many scholars who have accepted the latter's aesthetic avant-gardism, however, nonsynchronism is thought along a single temporal plane, such that both people and art can be nonsynchronous only to the extent that they are backward or advanced.

The politically and analytically reactionary potential of this sort of single-planed, nonsynchronous thinking is evident in development theories both geopolitical and aesthetic.[25] Perhaps the most notorious form of aesthetic developmentalism is the tendency to apply the Western aesthetic metanarrative of realism to modernism to postmodernism teleologically to non-Western (or, on occasion, ethnic-Western) literatures, inevitably casting the latter in "the role of repeating forms pioneered elsewhere in earlier times."[26] Beyond the more explicitly egregious manifestations which describe non-Western literature as "pre-modern" or paternalistically celebrate the overdue "emergence" of this or that national literature's "belated" modernism or postmodernism, this form of

---

[22] Ernst Bloch, "Nonsynchronism and the Obligation to Its Dialectics," trans. Mark Ritter, *New German Critique*, no. 11 (Spring 2017): 22. https://www.jstor.org/stable/487802.

[23] For a more extended consideration of Adorno's sense of "the modern" from which I have benefitted, see Peter Bürger, "The Decline of the Modern Age," trans. David J. Parent, *Telos* 1984, no. 62 (December 1984): 117-130, https://doi.org/10.3817/1284062117.

[24] Elizabeth Freeman, "Synchronic / Anachronic," in *Time: A Vocabulary of the Present*, eds. Joel Burges and Amy J. Elias (New York: New York UP, 2016), 137.

[25] For a thoroughgoing study of economic, cultural, and civilizational developmentalism, see Arturo Escobar, *Encountering Development: The Making and Unmaking of the Third World* (Princeton: Princeton UP, 2011).

[26] Jed Esty and Colleen Lye, "Peripheral Realisms Now," *Modern Language Quarterly* 73, no. 3 (September 2012): 269, https://doi.org/10.1215/00267929-1631397.

thought is evident in many contemporary theories of world literature, such as those of Franco Moretti and Pascale Casanova. Such theories imagine non-Western nations as resigned to belatedly and passively importing (and, to a limited extent, adapting) Western literary forms and producing variations of the same. It can also be observed in certain Marxist theorizations of totality which, because of their commitment to the determining influence of mode of production, ineluctably connect the uneven spread of capital to an uneven aesthetic development. When, for instance, Fredric Jameson called for extension of the literary canon to "often unmodern third-world texts" he not only homogenized all "Third World" novels as national allegories, but implied that the "Third World" represented a political-aesthetic situation that the West had, for better or worse, moved beyond.[27] Jameson's "romance of the residual" can be understood as a kind of post-colonial reconstruction of Adorno's (and, more generally, institutional modernism's) prioritization of the emergent, attesting to the distinctiveness of non-Western literature on grounds other than Western (post)modernism, but both obey a logic of temporal nonsynchronism that denies contemporaneity as such.[28]

The anthropologist Johannes Fabian puts forward the authoritative critique of single-planed nonsynchronism in the colonial context. What he called "the denial of coevalness" describes the "persistent and systematic tendency to place the referent(s) of anthropology in a Time other than the present of the producer of anthropological discourse."[29] Although his critique was aimed primarily at the Anglo-American and French anthropological traditions, the phenomenon he identifies—the anthropologist's description of non-Western cultures in terms that represent them as either historically and temporally prior (coded in such terms as "primitive," "traditional," and "uncivilized") or as existing in a permanent present (as if their present society is without history)—

---

[27] Fredric Jameson, "Third-World Literature in the Era of Multinational Capitalism," *Social Text*, no. 15 (Autumn 1986): 66, https://doi.org/10.2307/466493. For an early and influential critique of Jameson's essay, see Aijaz Ahmad, "Jameson's Rhetoric of Otherness and the 'National Allegory,'" *Social Text*, no. 17 (Autumn 1987): 3-25, https://doi.org/10.2307/466475. My discussion of Casanova, Moretti, and Jameson here is influenced by Shu-Mei Shih, "Global Literature and the Technologies of Recognition," *PMLA* 119, no. 1 (January 2004): 16-30, https://www.jstor.org/stable/1261482; Madhu Dubey, *Signs and Cities: Black Literary Postmodernism* (Chicago: University of Chicago Press, 2003); and Rey Chow, "Rereading Mandarin Ducks and Butterflies: A Response to the 'Postmodern' Condition," *Cultural Critique*, no. 5 (Winter 1986-1987): 69–93, https://doi.org/10.2307/1354357.

[28] Dubey, *Signs and Cities*, 22.

[29] Johannes Fabian, *Time and the Other: How Anthropology Makes its Object* (New York: Columbia UP, 1983), 31.

is pervasive not only in everyday language, but also, as we have seen, in cultural studies more generally.[30] Fabian as well recognized that such "allochronism" could work both ways, such that, as in Heidegger or Eliot, "the posited authenticity of a past (savage, tribal, peasant) serves to denounce an inauthentic present (the uprooted, *évolués*, acculturated)."[31]

Although such allochronism or nonsynchronism has not disappeared from the language and thinking of literary studies—Mark DiGiacomo has recently shown that an increasingly globalized modernist studies has still tended to deny the coevalness of African literature—there has been a conscious effort to mitigate the bigoted *effects* of nonsynchronism while retaining the premise of aesthetic developmentalism.[32] The philosopher Peter Osborne, for example, describes the present as "increasingly characterized by a coming together of *different but equally 'present'* temporalities or 'times,' a temporal unity in disjunction, or a *disjunctive unity of present times.*"[33] Because this unity is imaginary, however, Osborne defines "the contemporary" as "the fictive relational unity of the historical present."[34] Thus it is not, according to Osborne, so much that Fabian's critique is valid in itself, but that it has been socially actualized to the extent that the current historical conjuncture, with its increasing global interconnectedness, encourages this imaginary act of unity.[35]

If this conceptualization of the present is a somewhat useful attempt to think identity and difference at a theoretical level, it leads Osborne into familiar problems when he applies this notion of "the contemporary" to contemporary art. Just as Osborne had earlier elaborated on Adorno's nonsynchronic notion

---

[30] More recently, Dipesh Chakrabarty has elaborated on Fabian's critique with respect to historiography: the "archaic" exists within the contemporary "not as a remnant of another time but as something constitutive of the present." See Dipesh Chakrabarty, *Provincializing Europe: Postcolonial Thought and Historical Difference* (Princeton: Princeton UP, 2000), 251.

[31] Fabian, *Time and the Other*, 10.

[32] Mark DiGiacomo, "The Assertion of Coevalness: African Literature and Modernist Studies," *Modernism/Modernity* 24, no. 2 (April 2017): 245-262.

[33] Osborne, *Anywhere or Not at All*, 17, emphases in original. Harry Harootunian similarly characterizes "the history of our present as the unity of uneven temporalizations differentiating global geopolitical space." The exact point at which this becomes problematic is when "uneven" is generalized from the context of capitalist development to *history* writ large. See Harry Harootunian, "Theory's Empire: Reflections on a Vocation for Critical Inquiry," *Critical Inquiry* 30, no. 2 (Winter 2004): 401-402, https://doi.org/10.1086/421140.

[34] Osborne, *Anywhere or Not at All*, 26.

[35] Osborne, *Anywhere or Not at All*, 220.

of the modern in an essay titled "Modernity is a Qualitative, Not a Chronological, Category," he insists on designating contemporaneity as a qualitative category as well. While I cannot rehearse his entire argument here, Osborne's characterization of "the contemporary" as transnational leads to a description of contemporary art as defined by "de-bordering"—both the borders between artistic mediums and between national social spaces of art—and, finally, to the concise proposition that "contemporary art is post-conceptual art."[36]

Osborne's candidly exclusive definition of contemporary—"Not all art that is recently produced, or would call itself or be called by others 'contemporary,' can be understood to be contemporary in an art-critically significant sense"— participates in a tendency the art historian Donald Kuspit describes as "art history's attempt to control contemporaneity— and with that the temporal flow of art events—by stripping certain art events of their idiosyncrasy and incidentalness in the name of some absolute system of value."[37] Comparing the Venice Biennale of the 1960s with that of the twenty-first century, Kuspit finds that "the balance between the attempt to show as many samples as possible of the abundance of contemporary art and, on the other hand, to assert what will be art historically important to the future and so must be especially precious in the present, has tilted toward the latter and away from the former."[38] The effect is that of "predetermining art history" through the "selective inattention to other contemporary artists."[39] In denying the coevalness of contemporary art, Osborne and others transform the present into history and repudiate its very contemporaneity.[40] While the effect would ostensibly be the same if Osborne

---

[36] Osborne, *Anywhere or Not at All,* 28, 3.

[37] Osborne, *Anywhere or Not at All,* 2. Donald Kuspit, "The Contemporary and the Historical," *Artnet,* April 13, 2005, www.artnet.com/Magazine/features/kuspit/kuspit4-14-05.asp.

[38] Kuspit, "The Contemporary and the Historical."

[39] Kuspit, "The Contemporary and the Historical."

[40] Art historian Terry Smith has similarly attempted to define "truly" contemporary art in a way that avoids the denial of coevalness implicit in modernism. However, because this is an inherently contradictory task, Smith, like Osborne, is forced to effectively make nonsynchrony both the form *and the content* of "the contemporary": "...*contemporaneity consists precisely in the constant experience of radical disjunctures of perception, mismatching ways of seeing and valuing the same world, in the actual coincidence of asynchronous temporalities, in the jostling contingency of various cultural and social multiplicities, all thrown together in ways that highlight the fast-growing inequalities within and between them."* See Terry Smith, "Contemporary Art and Contemporaneity," 692, 703. As broad and potentially capacious as this definition may seem (and Smith indeed lists dozens of artists who exemplify different strains of his multidimensional and antinomous contemporaneity), the fact remains that artistic coevalness has been ironically denied

simply asserted that the major aesthetic movement of the present is post-conceptual art, his appropriation of "contemporary" aspires to revise the definition of contemporary art (and its study) from focusing on the chronological present to instead focusing on art that is qualitatively similar within a particular historical moment. It follows that some (chronologically) contemporary art is in fact uncontemporary (and thus not worthy of study as such) and the art of the future will at some point become post-contemporary. This seems to me an overly limited and terminologically unserviceable orientation toward the study of the literature of the present.

Such theories of historical nonsynchronism are, to be sure, immensely valuable tools for understanding the synchronic past diachronically. Because I already know certain broad differences between the literary culture of the 1920s, the 1950s, and the 1960s, I am able to read the literature of the 1950s both in terms of characteristics dominant in the 1920s that had lost the fullness of their hold without having disappeared (the imperative to create radically new aesthetic experiences through formal innovation, say) and of elements typical of the 1960s that were visible, but not yet representative of the 1950s (e.g., juxtaposition or conflation of various genres, high and low). A nonsynchronist perspective allows me to identify *Naked Lunch* and *The Recognitions* as "ahead of their time," *From Here to Eternity* as *démodé*, and *Invisible Man* as "truly" contemporary in the sense of coinciding closely with what we now recognize as The Fifties. Such a point of view allows us to add temporal dimension to the flatness of a past present, to recognize the past and the future which seem to be inherent in that present.

These nonsynchronous modes of reading the past have been challenged and supplemented in recent years, particularly in the work of queer theorists. Speaking of histories of sexuality, Peter Coviello criticizes what he terms the "anticipatory" approach to the past: "To read the sexually piquant moments of nineteenth-century American writing as finally anticipatory—as harbingers for the approach of, or as laying the groundwork for, a language of sexual identity and affiliation that would indeed arrive later—is to risk missing much of the story. It is to presume, for instance, that all roads lead to Rome . . ."[41] What scholars need to recognize, then, is that "the appearance of what we might want to call queer identity, or modern homosexual identity, was not a fate fixed in the stars, and was not the target toward which all emergences were speeding,

---

to the "less" contemporary artists and works that do not positively represent this definition of contemporaneity.

[41] Peter Coviello, *Tomorrow's Parties: Sex and the Untimely in Nineteenth-Century American Literature* (New York: New York UP, 2013), 15.

arrow-like, across the century."[42] Coviello thus calls for approaches to past presents that do not read that present diachronically, which is to say teleologically, selecting and interpreting phenomena according to the degree to which they appear to anticipate an actualized future.

If single-plane nonsynchronous approaches to the past are both highly useful and necessarily limited (and thus should be both critiqued and supplemented by other modes), they are considerably less conducive to an effective analysis of the present, our present. The reason this is so is embarrassingly simple: we do not and cannot know the future. The idea of the residual and the emergent, the retrograde and the avant-garde (in its nonsynchronic sense) are only legitimate analytical terms for describing the past; applied to the present, they are rhetorically valuable and phenomenally inevitable (as in Heidegger's retentions and protentions), but analytically inhibitive. To describe an element of the present as residual or emergent is to misread the present through the lens of a non-existent future.[43] Not only does this produce skewed analyses of the present (because the relative significance or historical value of phenomena are taken for granted), it also guarantees skewed analyses of future presents as they are read against their confirmation of or variance from a past future.

This is not to argue against speculation *tout court.* We can be almost certain that the problems already caused by changes in the global climate are going to continue and get rapidly worse; in consequence, many scholars are placing considerable emphasis on and investing in contemporary "cli-fiction" as a loose genre that will likely continue to grow in importance, at least until writers' studios are deluged. This investment makes sense, but it does not follow that we should define "contemporary" in such a way that fiction registering or engaging with the Anthropocene is *truly* contemporary and consequently that fiction which does not concern the environment is anachronous, un-contemporary. Likewise, I am not arguing against speculation *qua* speculation, but rather against analysis grounded by a telos, whether that telos is progressive formal innovation, a post-capitalist utopia, or a post-literary dystopia. This is also to contend that the concept of postmodernism produced bad analyses of

---

[42] Coviello, *Tomorrow's Parties*, 16.

[43] My argument here applies most particularly to the emergent and futural senses of the nonsynchronous. That being said, while we can indeed add dimension to the present by viewing it against the past, the notion of "the residual" implicitly assumes continued residual-ity. As an offhand example, the secularization thesis proffered in the late nineteenth century led to perceptions of both global and American religiosity as residual, perceptions based less on synchronic analysis than anticipatory speculation. We need new terms and concepts for thinking about the present's derivation and difference from the past.

past presents and that replacement concepts for postmodernism guarantee bad analyses of present presents. When we attempt to add temporal dimension to our own present, to differentiate chronologies and deny coevalness, we project our own imagined futures onto that present, and do not so much thicken it as dilute it.

I propose, then, that the "contemporary" in contemporary literature studies should be understood as a chronological, not a qualitative, category. The ongoing effort to attribute qualitative content to "the contemporary" should be resisted in order to maintain the term's deictic quality. A collection of realist short stories published by Random House in 2020, a formally experimental novel published by Dzanc in 2020, and a feminist autofiction published by South Korea's Changbi in 2020 should all, from the perspective of contemporary literature studies, qualify as equally contemporary.[44] The past or future do not inhere in any particular work or style or genre; the becoming or un-becoming we will one day recognize therein is a retrospective construction. If the objective of contemporary literature studies is to understand the literature of the present—and not just a narrow subset of new books, a proto-canon—it must begin from a position that does not preemptively schematize the literary field according to an implied telos. Speculation is unquestionably valuable, but only when informed by understanding.[45]

In order to make the chronological boundaries of contemporary literature studies more concrete, I would further suggest that contemporary literature be defined deictically as the literature published within the last fifteen years. In its indexical temporal designation, the field so defined would be distinguished from fields organized around historical periods and thus able to resist becoming identified with a past present, as with modernism. The proposal of fifteen years is not based on a theory that this is the normative temporal

---

[44] Undoubtedly, such an inclusive orientation has its own limits and I am not arguing against analytical distinctions, but rather the frequently *a priori* origins and immediacy of such distinctions. The reflexive drive to periodize and canonize (the one always implying the other) is, I think, an inheritance from historical literary scholarship that obscures the unique qualities of studying the present. For two insightful critiques of periodization's institutional hegemony, see Eric Hayot, "Against Periodization; Or, On Institutional Time," *New Literary History* 42, no. 4 (Autumn 2011): 739-756, https://www.jstor.org/stable/41328995; and Gerald Graff, "How Periods Erase History," *Common Knowledge* 21, no. 2 (April 2015): 177-183, https://doi.org/10.1215/0961754X-2872307.

[45] This should not be understood as forging a path to arrive at the elusive ideal of objectivity; the aim, ultimately, is to produce better and more self-aware, if less immediate, speculation by grounding such speculation in evidence-based knowledge rather than intuition or *idées recues*.

distance from a literary work or event at which point an object slides from contemporary to historical, present to past. Rather, it is more pragmatically founded in the classroom, wherein students in their late teens and early twenties might reasonably expect that the contemporary literature they read be contemporary with themselves rather than with their parents and teachers.[46] In *Camera Lucida*, Roland Barthes describes his frustration at being unable to truly recognize his mother in photographs from her youth. In contemplating the cause of this distance, Barthes surmises that "with regard to many of these photographs, it was History which separated me from them. Is History not simply that time when we were not born?"[47] In a certain phenomenal sense, it is indeed. And if contemporary literature is to be understood as literature that is not yet historical, the time frame of our students' lives offers a standard for a contemporary we all share—chronologically, if not qualitatively.

Works cited

Adorno, Theodor W. *Minima Moralia: Reflections on a Damaged Life*. Translated by E. F. N. Jephcott. New York: Verso, 2005.

Ahmad, Aijaz. "Jameson's Rhetoric of Otherness and the 'National Allegory.'" *Social Text*, no. 17 (Autumn 1987): 3-25. https://doi.org/10.2307/466475.

Alworth, David J. "Hip to Post45." *Contemporary Literature* 54, no. 3 (Fall 2013): 622-633. https://www.jstor.org/stable/43297925.

Barthes, Roland. *Camera Lucida: Reflections on Photography*. Translated by Richard Howard. New York: Hill and Wang, 2010.

Bloch, Ernst. "Nonsynchronism and the Obligation to Its Dialectics." Translated by Mark Ritter. *New German Critique*, no. 11 (Spring 2017): 22-38. https://www.jstor.org/stable/487802.

Bürger, Peter. "The Decline of the Modern Age." Translated by David J. Parent. *Telos* 1984, no. 62 (December 1984): 117-130. https://doi.org/10.3817/1284062117.

Chakrabarty, Dipesh. *Provincializing Europe: Postcolonial Thought and Historical Difference*. Princeton: Princeton UP, 2000.

Chihaya, Sarah, Joshua Kotin, and Kinohi Nishikawa. "Introduction: How To Be Now." *Post45* 2 (2019). https://post45.org/2019/07/introduction-how-to-be-now.

Chow, Rey. "Rereading Mandarin Ducks and Butterflies: A Response to the 'Postmodern' Condition." *Cultural Critique*, no. 5 (Winter 1986-1987): 69–93. https://doi.org/10.2307/1354357.

---

[46] Although he is speaking of realist fiction in particular, Gordon Hutner also argues for the importance of a student-centered notion of contemporary literature. See Gordon Hutner, "Historicizing the Contemporary: A Response to Amy Hungerford," *American Literary History* 20, no. 1 (Spring-Summer 2008): 420–24, https://doi.org/10.1093/alh/ajm048.

[47] Roland Barthes, *Camera Lucida: Reflections on Photography*, trans. Richard Howard (New York: Hill and Wang, 2010), 64.

Coviello, Peter. *Tomorrow's Parties: Sex and the Untimely in Nineteenth-Century American Literature*. New York: New York UP, 2013.

DiGiacomo, Mark. "The Assertion of Coevalness: African Literature and Modernist Studies." *Modernism/Modernity* 24, no. 2 (April 2017): 245–262. https://doi.org/10.1353/mod.2017.0020.

Dubey, Madhu. *Signs and Cities: Black Literary Postmodernism*. Chicago: University of Chicago Press, 2003.

Escobar, Arturo. *Encountering Development: The Making and Unmaking of the Third World*. Princeton: Princeton UP, 2011.

Esty, Jed, and Colleen Lye. "Peripheral Realisms Now." *Modern Language Quarterly* 73, no. 3 (September 2012): 269-288. https://doi.org/10.1215/00267929-1631397.

Fabian, Johannes. *Time and the Other: How Anthropology Makes its Object*. New York: Columbia UP, 1983.

Freeman, Elizabeth. "Synchronic / Anachronic." In *Time: A Vocabulary of the Present*, edited by Joel Burges and Amy J. Elias, 129-143. New York: New York UP, 2016.

Graff, Gerald. "How Periods Erase History." *Common Knowledge* 21, no. 2 (April 2015): 177-183. https://doi.org/10.1215/0961754X-2872307.

Harootunian, Harry. "Theory's Empire: Reflections on a Vocation for Critical Inquiry." *Critical Inquiry* 30, no. 2 (Winter 2004): 396-402. https://doi.org/10.1086/421140.

Hayot, Eric. "Against Periodization; Or, On Institutional Time." *New Literary History* 42, no. 4 (Autumn 2011): 739–756. https://www.jstor.org/stable/41328995.

Hoberek, Andrew, Samuel Cohen, Amy J. Elias, Mary Esteve, Matthew Hart, and David James. "Postmodern, Postwar, Contemporary: A Dialogue on the Field." In *Postmodern/Postwar—and After: Rethinking American Literature*, edited by Jason Gladstone, Andrew Hoberek, and Daniel Worden, 27-56. Iowa City: University of Iowa Press, 2016.

Hungerford, Amy. *Making Literature Now*. Stanford: Stanford UP, 2016.

———. "On the Period Formerly Known as Contemporary." *American Literary History* 20, no.1/2 (Spring-Summer 2008): 410-419. https://doi.org/10.1093/alh/ajm044.

Hutner, Gordon. "Historicizing the Contemporary: A Response to Amy Hungerford." *American Literary History* 20, no. 1 (Spring-Summer 2008): 420-424. https://doi.org/10.1093/alh/ajm048.

Hyde, Emily and Sarah Wasserman. "The Contemporary." *Literature Compass* 14, no. 9 (September 2017): 1-19. https://doi.org/10.1111/lic3.12411.

Jameson, Fredric. "Third-World Literature in the Era of Multinational Capitalism." *Social Text*, no. 15 (Autumn 1986): 65-88. https://doi.org/10.2307/466493.

Kirby, Alan. *Digimodernism: How New Technologies Dismantle the Postmodern and Reconfigure Our Culture*. New York: Continuum, 2009.

Kuspit, Donald. "The Contemporary and the Historical." *Artnet*, April 13, 2005. www.artnet.com /Magazine/features/kuspit/kuspit4-14-05.asp.

Martin, Theodore. *Contemporary Drift: Genre, Historicism, and the Problem of the Present*. New York: Columbia UP, 2017.

———. "Contemporary, Inc." *Representations* 142 (Spring 2018): 124-144. https://doi.org/10.1525/rep.2018.142.1.124.

Moraru, Christian. *Cosmodernism: American Narrative, Late Globalization, and the New Cultural Imaginary.* Ann Arbor: University of Michigan Press, 2011.

Nealon, Jeffrey T. *Post-Postmodernism; Or, the Cultural Logic of Just-in-Time Capitalism.* Stanford: Stanford UP, 2012.

North, Michael. *What Is the Present?* Princeton: Princeton UP, 2018.

Osborne, Peter. *Anywhere or Not at All: Philosophy of Contemporary Art.* New York: Verso, 2013.

Shih, Shu-Mei. "Global Literature and the Technologies of Recognition." *PMLA* 119, no. 1 (January 2004): 16-30. http://www.jstor.org/stable/1261482.

Smith, Terry. "Contemporary Art and Contemporaneity." *Critical Inquiry* 32, no. 4 (Summer 2006): 681-707. https://doi.org/10.1086/508087.

Williams, Raymond. *Keywords: A Vocabulary of Culture and Society.* Oxford: Oxford UP, 2015.

Chapter 2

"Contemporary" comparisons: *The Silent Minaret* at the intersection of the "post" debates

Amanda Lagji

Pitzer College

Abstract

This chapter argues that South African writer Ishtiyaq Shukri's 2005 novel *The Silent Minaret* is a "contemporary" novel par excellence for how the various lenses of the contemporary converge and shape not only its thematic interests, but also its form. I track how the novel both expands our account of 9/11 fiction, for example, and reveals the temporal preoccupations and the colonial unconscious of "the contemporary." The novel's formal mechanisms amplify characteristics of both post-1989 and post-9/11 texts, and I demonstrate how the novel advances a view of the time-space dimension of the contemporary, through its deployment of what I call the aesthetics of juxtaposition to produce Issa as a truly "contemporary" protagonist. Where Emily Hyde and Sarah Wasserman see world literature moving "away from a basis in spatial extension, which offers no particular theory of the contemporary, to a basis in temporality, which may," I argue that The Silent Minaret's theory of the contemporary involves both space and time. As I will demonstrate, the juxtaposition of South African apartheid with the Israeli occupation of Palestine in the novel's final pages is integral to this vision.

Keywords: 9/11 Fiction; Shukri, Ishtiyaq; The Silent Minaret; Apartheid Literature; World Literature

***

Overview

When, where, and what is the contemporary? As Emily Hyde and Sarah Wasserman observe in their 2017 essay, "The Contemporary," whether we periodize the contemporary as post-45 or post-89, American literature is disproportionately represented in literary studies.[1] This "US-centric" bias, they note, remains even when the frame is expanded to include so-called "global" or "world literature" traditions. In his important 2017 study, *Contemporary Drift*, Theodore Martin sidesteps these questions by viewing "the contemporary not as a self-evident historical period but as a conceptual problem."[2] In many of the recent accounts of the contemporary, the postcolonial is either absent (as both theoretical framework and canon of literature) or eschewed in favor of global or world literature. Treasa De Loughry, for example, separates "global fictions" from "world literature" on the basis of "the latter's emergence from comparative literary studies," and further distinguishes global fiction from postcolonial literature, which in her view "require the contextuality of local immiseration or decolonial struggles and require less meta-translation of national conditions or local histories."[3] Indeed, as the 2019 contributions to the "Forms of the Global Anglophone" forum in *Post45*'s "Contemporaries" series attests, distinguishing between what is properly global or postcolonial, not to mention transnational or "world," is a messy endeavor.[4]

In the end, this entanglement may be one of the most salient features of both contemporary criticism and contemporary literature. The continued proliferations of "posts" attached to contemporary literature—from post-45 and post-89, to postwar or postcolonial, to post-9/11—appears to underscore Hyde and Wasserman's claim that both criticism and fiction evince "a recurrent concern with time and temporality."[5] In my own contribution to these debates, I argue that South African writer Ishtiyaq Shukri's 2005 novel *The Silent Minaret* is a "contemporary" novel *par excellence* in how the various lenses of the contemporary converge and shape not only its thematic interests, but also its form. Thus, in this chapter, I am less interested in the when, where, and what of the contemporary, than in the how—specifically how *The Silent Minaret* uncovers what Mitchum Huehls describes as the "political value of time" of the

---

[1] Emily Hyde and Sarah Wasserman, "The Contemporary," *Literature Compass* 14, no. 9 (September 2017): 2, https://doi.org/10.1111/lic3.12411.

[2] Theodore Martin, *Contemporary Drift: Genre, Historicism, and the Problem of the Present* (New York: Columbia UP, 2017), 2.

[3] Treasa De Loughry, *The Global Novel and Capitalism in Crisis: Contemporary Literary Narratives* (New York: Palgrave Macmillan, 2020), 2, 28-29.

[4] Nasia Anam, et al., "Forms of the Global Anglophone," *Post45*, February 22, 2019, https://post45.org/sections/contemporaries/global-anglophone/.

[5] Hyde and Wasserman, "The Contemporary," 3.

contemporary in the wake of various "posts."[6] In addition to its postcolonial investments, the novel is also pointedly a post-apartheid novel and work of contemporary South African fiction. To complicate its position in contemporary literature further, Shukri's novel is *also* a work of post-9/11 fiction, following the disappearance of its protagonist Issa in London after he watches the bombing of Baghdad in distress.

By categorizing the novel as contemporary, postcolonial, post-apartheid, and post-9/11 specifically, I do not intend to suggest that these aforementioned categories are either self-evident or uncontroversial. Instead, I will track how the novel both fits and revises these various categorizations, expanding our account of 9/11 fiction, for example, and revealing the temporal preoccupations and the colonial unconscious of "the contemporary." To both narrow and anchor my focus for the purposes of this chapter, my investigation of how *The Silent Minaret* embeds the preoccupations of the contemporary will examine how the novel's formal mechanisms amplify characteristics of both post-1989 and post-9/11 texts, how the novel advances a view of the time-space dimension of the contemporary, and finally how the novel employs what I call the aesthetics of juxtaposition to produce Issa as a truly "contemporary" protagonist. Where Hyde and Wasserman see world literature moving "away from a basis in spatial extension, which offers no particular theory of the contemporary, to a basis in temporality, which may," I argue that *The Silent Minaret*'s theory of the contemporary involves *both* space and time.[7] As I will demonstrate, the juxtaposition of South African apartheid with the Israeli occupation of Palestine in the novel's final pages is integral to this vision.

The long history of the contemporary

The contemporary is admittedly a slippery temporal designation, as time progresses and the present moves quickly into the more and more distant past. In literary scholarship, as Hyde and Wasserman's useful survey shows, scholars sometimes periodize the contemporary as beginning in 1945, while others "delineate a shorter span that begins sometime around 1980," but regardless of when we begin, contemporary novels, they find, "often revisit and revise the past through explicitly formal means and ...they do this not to break from that past but to interrogate its continuities with the present."[8] These novels "often

---

[6] Mitchum Huehls, *Qualified Hope: A Postmodern Politics of Time* (Columbus: Ohio State UP, 2009), 4.

[7] Hyde and Wasserman, "The Contemporary," 8.

[8] Hyde and Wasserman, "The Contemporary," 3, 11.

invoke multiple futures and timescales, staging the multiplicity and discrepancy of those times through formal means."[9] What signals the contemporaneousness of a given text, then, is equally what it says about the present moment *and* how it calls forth the afterlives of the past to make sense of this present. To put it another way, the contemporary appears to be less about breaks and disjuncture than about temporal entanglements and palimpsests.

A subset of contemporary literature, post-9/11 fiction—especially those texts whose representations of terror expand beyond the immediate American response and experience—insists on the long history of contemporary terror. In *Plotting Justice* (2012), Georgiana Banita analyzes a range of texts that "recontextualize the terrorist attacks as one in a series of twentieth-century events (from the Holocaust to the Balkan civil war) that have challenged our assumptions about living with cruelty and terror."[10] As we will see, the cruelty and terror that *The Silent Minaret* traces begins with the Dutch East India Company's incarceration of political dissidents on the South African Cape centuries ago, and continues through the South African apartheid regime, the contemporary War on Terror, and finally, occupied Palestine. This interrogation of global history, and the form it takes in Shukri's text, encourages us to consider the ways that new categorizations of world literature, as well as specifically post-9/11 literature, dovetail in the novel's representation of South African history and the afterlives of colonial forms of imprisonment in our contemporary times. In continuing to use the term "post-9/11," I follow Pei-Chen Liao's lead in his book, *Post-9/11 South Asian Diasporic Fiction*, where he asserts that his "special use of the term" understands "the meaning of 'post-' as 'against' the uniqueness of 9/11, if not anti-9/11."[11] Although Liao does not analyze *The Silent Minaret*, his characterization of post-9/11 South Asian diasporic fiction seems to fit: these texts "juxtapose the violence inherent in both 9/11 and the War on Terror with sexual and racial discrimination, ethnic cleansing, the Holocaust, the anti-immigration movement, and global capitalism… [in order to] rethink the broader meanings of 9/11 and the War on Terror in light of the ambivalent link between violence and identity."[12] Later in this chapter, I

---

[9] Hyde and Wasserman, "The Contemporary," 11.

[10] Georgiana Banita, *Plotting Justice: Narrative Ethics and Literary Culture after 9/11* (Lincoln: University of Nebraska Press, 2012), 1. While Banita aims "to identify a stronger, more varied 9/11 literary canon than has been acknowledged so far" (15), I note that many of the authors she studies remain white and/or American.

[11] Pei-Chen Liao, *"Post"-9/11 South Asian Diasporic Fiction: Uncanny Terror* (New York: Palgrave Macmillan, 2013), 1.

[12] Liao, *"Post"-9/11 South Asian Diasporic Fiction*, 155.

will return to how the comparison between South Africa and Palestine in *The Silent Minaret* works against the exceptionalism and uniqueness in the sense that Liao uses "post." For now, I note that taken together, Banita and Liao, along with Hyde and Wasserman, suggest that contemporary 9/11 fiction deploys formal innovations to foreground persistent pasts and to dissuade us from a too-easy association of the contemporary with the utterly new and exceptional.

In terms of form and structure, *The Silent Minaret* is notable for its heteroglossic investigation of Issa's disappearance. On March 20, 2003, Issa Shamsuddin, the novel's missing central character, watches the United States bomb Baghdad as part of its expanded War on Terror. As recounted by Issa's friend Katinka, this moment marks the last time that Issa is seen by his friends before he disappears. The novel is comprised of flashbacks, memories, and conversations between Issa's friends and family as they try to understand where he might have gone and for what reasons. Both possibilities—that he has decided to disappear to the Middle East to fight, radicalized by the broadcast of the United States' shock-and-awe campaign, or that he has been disappeared by the UK or US governments, swept up in counter-terror racial profiling—are plausible. Over the course of the novel, we learn that Issa had been active in the armed wing of the ANC during the apartheid struggle and other South African political exiles warn Issa's mother that for people like Issa, the 'struggle' is never over. The novel opens from the perspective of Issa's downstairs neighbor, an elderly woman named Frances. But we also get third- and first-person narration from Kagiso's perspective; he is Issa's brother who goes to London to find answers as well as to pack up Issa's room. There are also Ma Vasinthe and Ma Gloria, Issa and Kagiso's mothers, respectively. Finally, we also see Issa's life through Katinka's eyes; she is the Afrikaner hitchhiker that Kagiso and Issa pick up on their way to Cape Town to celebrate Nelson Mandela's release. Interspersed and incorporated throughout the text are newspaper clippings, text messages, a missing persons poster, excerpts from the TRC report, history books, and Issa's dissertation. Many of the pieces of Issa's life in South Africa and in London are related through characters' memories or through dialogue between characters as they reflect on what might have caused Issa's disappearance.

By moving back and forth between the terror of apartheid and the War on Terror, Shukri allows echoes of oppression to reverberate—not to collapse differences, but to caution against complacency that would allow these histories to repeat. In Jane Poyner's view, this formal strategy "refuse[s] to foreclose important questions that connect the colonial past with the rhetoric of today."[13] The cliché, "one man's terrorist is another man's freedom fighter," resonates with South Africa's past especially, as Nelson Mandela was famously "branded a terrorist by western world leaders like Reagan, Thatcher and Dick Cheney."[14] In her brief survey of the application of the word "terrorism" from eighteenth-century France to the present, Poyner observes that "the rhetoric of 'terror'...has been cynically employed by hegemonic states to maintain strategic interests in the (post)colonies in the guise of moral right."[15] Shukri's novel encourages us to trace the images and practices of contemporary terror back even further, as Issa's research connects "the Dutch occupation of the Cape to the War on Terror," because both "are iterations of restricting mobility and freedom and are constituted in the ubiquity of a polarizing suspicion of others."[16]

The formal mechanisms through which *The Silent Minaret* recasts post-9/11 culture, history, and politics reflect the trends that Debjani Ganguly identifies in post-1989 global novels. She argues that "a new kind of novel as a global literary form emerged at the conjuncture of three critical phenomena: the geopolitics of war and violence since the end of the cold war; hyperconnectivity through advances in information technology; and the emergence of a new humanitarian sensibility in a context where suffering has a presence in everyday life through the immediacy of digital images."[17] Following Ganguly, I contend that the global novel "evinces a capacity...to imagine the human condition on a scale larger than ever before in history and certainly beyond national and regional configurations."[18] Building from these post-1989 and post-9/11 frameworks for reading contemporary novels, I offer two propositions: 1) Shukri's *The Silent Minaret* marks a change in literature—not simply South African or African literature, but World Literature—in its orientation and depiction of the post-9/11 world from a global South African perspective. And

---

[13] Jane Poyner, "Cosmopolitanism and Fictions of 'Terror': Zoë Wicomb's *David's Story* and Ishtiyaq Shukri's *The Silent Minaret*," *Safundi: The Journal of South African and American Studies* 12, no. 3-4 (2011): 313, https://doi.org/10.1080/17533171.2011.586832.

[14] Elleke Boehmer, "Postcolonial Terrorist: The Example of Nelson Mandela," *Parallax* 11, no. 4 (August 2005): 46, https://doi.org/10.1080/13534640500331666.

[15] Poyner, "Cosmopolitanism and Fictions of 'Terror,'" 314.

[16] Cleo Beth Theron, "Reconstructing the Past, Deconstructing the Other: Redefining Cultural Identity Through History and Memory in Ishtiyaq Shukri's *The Silent Minaret*," *English Studies in Africa* 57, no. 2 (2014): 47, https://doi.org/10.1080/00138398.2014.963283.

[17] Debjani Ganguly, *This Thing Called the World: The Contemporary Novel as Global Form* (Durham: Duke UP, 2016), 1.

[18] Ganguly, *This Thing Called the World*, 2.

2) Shukri's novel, when placed in the context of other, more canonical post-9/11 novels, illuminates several changes in that field as well. The novel presents 9/11 and the War on Terror as global events that contain the afterlives of colonial projects and neo-imperial endeavors. This critical and historical view of terror across the twentieth century and beyond is not only an essential counterpoint to American-centric literary depictions of global terrorism, but also exemplifies the contemporary's emphasis on temporality and history.

Entangled temporalities

Even as *The Silent Minaret* addresses the post-apartheid, postcolonial, and post-9/11 contemporary moment, Shukri clearly marks these "posts" as after, but *not* beyond. This is an important distinction; rather than viewing temporal epochs as discrete periods, as some attempts at categorizing the contemporary assume, the novel directly confronts this logic by showing deep entanglements. Fiction, Mitchum Huehls suggests, is particularly well-positioned to "expan[d] the form of temporal experience," and "populat[e] and temporaliz[e] the present with the past," thereby "expand[ing] our ability to conceive the political value of time."[19] I would add that analyzing contemporary fiction allows us to identify the emergent political value of the slippery contemporary itself, where the present is recast as enmeshed with the past. As Theodore Martin opines, the contemporary as a "critical concept... compels us to think, above all, about the politics of how we think about the present," a present which is "inseparable from the historically determined and politically motivated ways we choose to divide the present from the past." [20] In this way, *The Silent Minaret's* refusal to divide the present from the past indexes its own temporal politics of entanglement. This entanglement is not simply a statement of description, but also an act of radical reimagining. The "best models of temporal politics," Huehls concludes, "are those that integrate and intertwine multiple panels of time to produce unique temporal forms that incite us to think about politics in radically new ways."[21] Writing explicitly on fiction published since 2000, Andrzej Gąsiorek and David James draw on Roger Luckhurst's survey of Iraq War fiction and agree that the "multiple overlays of war times" employed by these fictions—including the "polytemporal overlay of prior wars on the

---

[19] Huehls, *Qualified Hope*, 4.
[20] Martin, *Contemporary Drift*, 5.
[21] Huehls, *Qualified Hope*, 195.

experience of Iraq"—permits us to "grasp our contemporary condition."[22] In addition to palimpsest-like overlays of prior wars and armed struggles, *The Silent Minaret* expands these concerns to include the banality of coloniality and everyday violence.

One of the ways that Shukri's characters distinguish the entangled time-space of the contemporary is through the asymmetrical violence of the War on Terror. In the Baghdad Café in London, Issa watches the United States' bombing of the "real" Baghdad in horror while his PhD dissertation in history lies open-faced on the café table. In language that explodes the temporal distance between then and now, Shukri notes that "time buckled, history flipped and the 17th century became indistinguishable from the 21st."[23] Overwhelmed by current events, Issa "found it impossible to drag himself from the present and into the past. He was no longer able to distinguish between the two."[24] Though Issa is certainly powerfully affected by the real-time broadcast of the bombing occurring elsewhere, Frances' proclamation that war is "no longer reciprocal" introduces another important space-time dimension to the experience of contemporary warfare. Whereas the distribution of viral images and videos of war circulate globally, the cost and risk of war is not distributed equally. At Christmas time, Frances reflects on this new state of affairs. She asks, "I wonder how many of the mongers would still support this war if there were the possibility of retaliation. But there isn't [....] Now the world's strongest countries bomb its poorest. Where's the honour in that?"[25]

In the years since *The Silent Minaret* was published, the unequal experiences of citizens in countries at war has only deepened, especially given the United States' expansive use of drone warfare in recent years. While Ganguly, I believe, accurately depicts the immediacy of suffering wrought by advances in technology and increasing hyperconnectivity, she does not address to the same extent the ways that the same technology conducts a simultaneously *distancing* process—not only removing the suffering, often civilian body from the immediate experience of the potential witnesses, but also removing the cost of war and the risks of war from the daily lives of the civilians in the more powerful country. Explaining how his term "interwar" comprises both senses

---

[22] Andrzej Gąsiorek and David James, "Introduction: Fiction Since 2000: Postmillennial Commitments," *Contemporary Literature* 53, no. 4 (Winter 2012): 621, https://www.jstor.org/stable/41819530.

[23] Ishtiyaq Shukri, *The Silent Minaret* (Johannesburg: Jacana, 2005), 70.

[24] Shukri, *The Silent Minaret*, 67.

[25] Shukri, *The Silent Minaret*, 165.

of being in between and in the midst of war, Paul Saint-Amour notes that "what one subject, community, or population experiences as an interval of peace another may experience as a time of intermittent or even continuous violence, whether in the shape of small wars, colonial occupation and policing, anticolonial uprising, civil war, or the psychic violence of war-anticipation."[26] With reference to the War on Terror specifically, Saint-Amour stresses that "technological asymmetries" like drone strikes:

> put target and targeter not just in vastly different time zones but also in disparate temporalities vis-a-vis war and peace. [...] Asymmetric in intensity and totality as well as in temporality: for where the drone attack is partial for the remote operator, the executive, and the citizenry in whose name the strike occurs, it is total for the figures down below, on the receiving end of the bombs. These antinomies of law and force, partiality and totality, space and time, are among the basic elements of our perpetual interwar. Violence for now is constant; only war is intermittent.[27]

Here, Saint-Amour suggestively tracks the larger continuities of waging war across the post-45 and continuing "post" moments. Shukri's novel dwells on the relationship between an immediate sense of time and a disparate sense of space, resisting the time-space compression that David Harvey claims characterizes late capitalism and pointing to the ways that space is both compressed *and* expanded according to the interests of hegemonic states.[28]

Though Frances aptly anticipates Saint-Amour's later analysis of the asymmetries of war, in *The Silent Minaret*, Shukri alludes to the Finsbury Park Mosque incident in London to show how violence is also perpetrated unevenly or asymmetrically even at "home." The chapter, titled "Finsbury Mosque," contains flashbacks to Issa's university days, as South African police and helicopters bear down on anti-apartheid activists. In the present moment, helicopters in London move in on the mosque in an alleged anti-terrorist raid.[29] The images of police helicopters transport him back in time and he remembers how the police invaded the campus to find anti-apartheid demonstrators. After finding several doors to various departments locked, Issa finds refuge in his

---

[26] Paul K. Saint-Amour, *Tense Future: Modernism, Total War, Encyclopedic Form* (Oxford: Oxford UP, 2015), 306.

[27] Saint-Amour, *Tense Future*, 312.

[28] David Harvey, "Time-Space Compression and the Postmodern Condition," in *Modernity: Critical Concepts*, ed. Malcom Waters, IV (London: Routledge, 1999), 98-118.

[29] Shukri, *The Silent Minaret*, 197.

college's History Department. History, we know, is also the discipline in which Issa is writing his PhD, but, primed by the mosque raid, Issa's studies have become indistinguishable from what he observes in the present. As mentioned above, the night Issa disappears, he watches the bombing of Baghdad on a giant TV, while "time buckled, history flipped, and the 17th century became indistinguishable from the 21st [....] He was no longer able to distinguish between the two."[30] He texts Katinka to join him, writing, "Kids r dying here."[31] I want to pause on this phrase, and in particular, note the "here" that concludes the sentence. It is not the case that kids are dying "here," the here of the café from which Issa writes his text message, and the same café at which Katinka soon joins him. The *here* is Baghdad, made more immediate not only through the TV screens, but also through the other inhabitants of the café for whom Baghdad is home. As Issa's waiter watches the "ancient city [his hometown]...decimated [and] smouldering," he does not notice Issa's "silent departure; only closes his welling eyes and inhales..."[32] Combined with his earlier observation that the past and present have become indistinguishable, Issa's statements reflect a juxtaposition of here and there that culminates in the collapse of space and time. A tapestry of flashbacks and echoes, the Finsbury Mosque chapter weaves together Issa's history dissertation about the "procedures of dispossession and domination implemented [in the Cape] in the fifteenth century [that] would be repeated around the globe for the rest of the millennium, and then again at the start of this new millennium,"[33] Issa's memories of police violence against anti-apartheid protestors, and his current reactions to how the United States and Britain wage the War on Terror. In effect, Shukri produces a vivid account of how the "contemporary" remains entangled in the temporalities of the past, the afterlives of colonialism, and the perpetuation of asymmetrical violence.

Contemporary comparisons: the aesthetics of juxtaposition

While the previous section emphasized the enduring past in the contemporary present, in this section, I turn to how Shukri expands his analysis of the present itself by juxtaposing formations of apartheid in South Africa and Palestine. Both Issa, of Indian descent, and his friend Katinka, a white Afrikaner, remark on the cycles of terror that shape the present. Though critics from various disciplines have often drawn comparisons between apartheid-South Africa and present-

---

[30] Shukri, *The Silent Minaret*, 70.

[31] Shukri, *The Silent Minaret*, 218.

[32] Shukri, *The Silent Minaret*, 75.

[33] Shukri, *The Silent Minaret*, 65.

day Israel and Palestine, literary critics tend not to focus on the import of *The Silent Minaret*'s Palestine sections. When critics *have* discussed these passages, they are largely subsumed in discussions of the novel's transnational aesthetics or stand-in from the Islamic world more broadly. In contrast, in this section, I want to address head-on the suggestive links the novel produces between human rights abuses in South Africa and the occupied Palestinian territories— especially the production of walls and boundaries in both settings—and Shukri's use of what I call the aesthetics of juxtaposition in service of the general politics of comparison. Thus, I expand my analysis of the contemporary beyond time and temporality to consider how the novel frames contemporary space. When apartheid South Africa and contemporary Israel have been discussed together, critics tend to be concerned about the real differences in each country's production of separateness or apartness. I will begin first by laying the groundwork for comparison and analogy *outside* the fiction, with a specific focus on law and human rights, and then I will layer Shukri's portrayal and use of the aesthetics of juxtaposition onto this groundwork. By way of conclusion, I will summarize what "work" the aesthetics of juxtaposition accomplish in the novel toward framing the present's historical moment, legitimizing struggle and resistance, demonstrating continuities across terror regimes, and perhaps writing the end of the occupation of Palestine.

The comparison of life under South African apartheid and life under Israeli governments is one that not only Palestinians, but also prominent South Africans have famously made, including Archbishop Desmond Tutu, who observes that his experience in South Africa "bears such remarkable parallels with the struggle of the Palestinian people for their freedom from the oppression and injustice imposed on them by successive Israeli governments."[34] In the 2015 collection *Apartheid Israel: The Politics of an Analogy*, editors Jon Soske and Sean Jacobs argue that analogies between South Africa and Israel help to highlight the colonial origins and settler project of consolidating a nation-state through "expropriation and expulsion."[35] While they admit that "no historical analogy is ever exact," they also note that "[t]he apartheid analogy also illuminates the circularity of Israeli's security argument: since occupation and settlement generate resistance, there can be no resolution to the 'conflict' short of Israel's withdrawal from the occupied territories and the

---

[34] Desmond Tutu, "Foreword BDS," in *Generation Palestine: Voices from the Boycott, Divestment and Sanctions Movement*, ed. Rich Wiles (London: Pluto Press, 2013), xiii.

[35] Jon Soske and Sean Jacobs, "Apartheid/Hafrada: South Africa, Israel, and the Politics of Historical Comparison," in *Apartheid Israel: The Politics of an Analogy*, eds. Jon Soske and Sean Jacobs (Chicago: Haymarket Books, 2015), 13.

dismantling of its colonizing infrastructure."[36] The collection as a whole aims "to make the work of comparison explicit, therefore creating open spaces for critical self-reflection rather than 'objectively' tallying similarities and differences."[37]

The editors' observation raises an important point: more than the tallying of similarities and differences, what work can the practice of comparison accomplish? In her article "The Work of Comparison: Israel/Palestine and Apartheid," the anthropologist Julie Peteet argues that the "work of comparison is the space it opens for new ways of conceptualizing and critiquing standard formulations of exceptionalism."[38] In this way, she extends Soske and Jacob's point that comparisons between South Africa and Israel open up space for debate and reflection, and notes that the *political* work the comparison accomplishes, in this case, is to de-exceptionalize and de-nationalize particular histories by locating them "in more expansive fields of analysis."[39] Peteet, like every other scholar working on comparisons between Israel and Africa in good faith, acknowledges the real differences between the histories, geographies, and peoples of the two; however, her point is that a comparative framework can accommodate "both specificity and uniqueness," and that "pinpointing difference does not invalidate comparison as a method of inquiry."[40] Taken together, if the work of comparison opens up space for critical, reflective critique, resists exceptionalism, *and* works toward legitimizing the Palestinian liberation struggle, we might then ask, where does Shukri's novel fit in? What might literary forms uniquely offer as an aesthetic representation or critique? The work of comparison resonates with Liao's efforts, cited above, to de-exceptionalize the uniqueness of 9/11 in his own deployment of "post-9/11" as a critical framework. This critical use of "post"—as against uniqueness— is manifested in the method of comparison and, as I will show below, in the aesthetics of juxtaposition that Shukri employs.

Before continuing further, I want to reiterate, as Soske and Jacobs do, that "in drawing a comparison between the two cases, the apartheid analogy is clearly targeting a set of *state* practices and policies—not the Israeli Jewish population

---

[36] Soske and Jacobs, "Apartheid/Hafrada," 12-13.

[37] Soske and Jacobs, "Apartheid/Hafrada," 16.

[38] Julie Peteet, "The Work of Comparison: Israel/Palestine and Apartheid," *Anthropological Quarterly* 89, no. 1 (Winter 2016): 249, https://jstor.org/stable/43955521.

[39] Peteet, "The Work of Comparison," 245.

[40] Peteet, "The Work of Comparison," 254.

as a group of people."[41] Further, while *The Silent Minaret* forges connections and comparisons between the experiences of human rights violations as well as everyday forms of oppression between Palestine and South Africa, when Israeli policies are characterized as apartheid policies by the BDS movement, they are "*not* making a direct analogy with the South African regime," but rather asserting that "Israeli policies should be condemned as the crime of apartheid under international law."[42] International law professor Richard Falk, who also served as a UN special Rapporteur on human rights in the Palestinian territories, clarifies that "international law treats apartheid as a universal crime, and not one that necessarily resembles the forms of drastic discrimination that prevailed in South Africa."[43] The 1975 International Convention on the Suppression and Punishment of the Crime of Apartheid defines apartheid as "inhuman acts for the purpose of establishing and maintaining domination by one racial group of persons over any other racial group and systematically oppressing them."[44] When I talk about the politics of comparison, then, I am not referring to the question of whether Israeli policies constitute apartheid under international law; that is a question that need not be answered by analogy with South Africa, but rather under the rubric of the universal law itself. As Suren Pillay, an anthropologist with the Center for Humanities Research at the University of the Western Cape observes, the South Africa and Israeli analogy is a "powerful one," which "put[s] an internationally accepted crime against humanity," that is South African apartheid, "alongside one that struggles to be accepted as a legitimate struggle from powerful Western states."[45]

Beyond juxtaposing Issa's participation in the anti-apartheid struggle with Katinka's experiences in the West Bank, Katinka explicitly invites the comparison between the occupied Palestinian territories and South Africa's apartheid-era Bantustans when she invites Kagiso to witness and document life there behind the wall. She writes to him, "So, 'Mr. Best Documentary Film Maker 2004,' when you've lapped up the praise and feel ready for your next assignment, why not

---

[41] Soske and Jacobs, "Apartheid/Hafrada," 17, my emphasis.

[42] Soske and Jacobs, "Apartheid/Hafrada," 11.

[43] Richard Falk, "International Law, Apartheid and Israeli Responses to BDS," in *Generation Palestine: Voices from the Boycott, Divestment and Sanctions Movement*, ed. Rich Wiles (London: Pluto Press, 2013), 88-89.

[44] Falk, "International Law, Apartheid and Israeli Responses to BDS," 89.

[45] Suren Pillay, "Checkpoints and Counterpoints: Edward Said and the Question of Apartheid," in *Apartheid Israel: The Politics of an Analogy*, eds. Jon Soske and Sean Jacobs (Chicago: Haymarket Books, 2015), 108.

bring your cameras here? But be warned. It's far more horrendous than anything you've seen in the homelands..."[46] Although Shukri concludes the novel with Katinka in the West Bank, living in the shadow of the Apartheid Wall, Shukri himself had not visited Palestine until after the publication of *The Silent Minaret*. In an essay titled "Palestine Journey," Shukri remarks that Palestinians themselves find comparative frameworks useful for understanding their own situation, "draw[ing] comparisons between the permits they are forced to carry and the passbooks for which South Africa was notorious. They see similarities between the map of their shrinking terrain and the mass of South Africa's former Bantustans."[47] In the debate over the apartheid analogy, I find that most critics do not spend time considering how the comparative framework works *for* Palestinians to articulate their hopes for international pressure on Israeli apartheid policies. Analogy is a form of comparative meaning-making, producing new ways of understanding *both* objects under comparison. The novel form both utilizes the power of analogy through the aesthetics of juxtaposition, bringing Palestine, South Africa, and the US-led War on Terror into close proximity, and also comments on its own project through extracts of Issa's dissertation. Issa writes, "*Reading is inevitably a complex, comparative process. A novel in in particular, if it is not to be read reductively as an item of socio-political evidence, involves the reader with itself not only because of its writer's skill but because of all other novels. All novels belong to a family, and any reader of novels is a reader of this complex family to which they all belong.*"[48]

Shukri underscores the complex, comparative process of reading by embedding a range of other texts and documents, movies, music, and allusions to fiction throughout the novel. But I would argue that the connections and comparisons he makes across time, between the Dutch settlement of the Cape, South African apartheid, the War on Terror, and contemporary life in the West Bank, suggest to us that we might read these geographies and histories, to trope on Issa's dissertation, through a complex, comparative process as well—not to read them reductively as an item of socio-political evidence, but because they relate to one another through the family resemblance of dispossession, removal, and boundaries. Importantly, one link between the seemingly disparate locales of the Dutch settlement of the Cape, later South African apartheid, and life in the West Bank is the manipulation of space.

---

[46] Shukri, *The Silent Minaret*, 273.

[47] Ishtiyaq Shukri, "Palestine Journey," in *Apartheid Israel: The Politics of an Analogy*, eds. Sean Jacobs and Jon Soske (Chicago: Haymarket Books, 2015), 27.

[48] Shukri, *The Silent Minaret*, 166.

For Issa, the process of dispossession that begins with the European exploration of the Cape of Good Hope is "universally and eternally pertinent."[49] He notes that the "procedures of dispossession and domination implemented here in the fifteenth century would be repeated around the globe for the rest of the millennium, and then again at the start of this new millennium."[50] In "Palestine Journey," Shukri recounts that in 1660, the "Dutch settlers planted [a] wild almond hedge...making it the first official boundary between the Cape Colony and the indigenous Khoi population. From the moment it took root, so too did the notion of division, which flourished to become the most defining feature of our society for the next 350 years."[51] In the patterns of dispossession since the colonization of space is linked with a complementary colonization of time. While implicit in the homelands policy in South Africa, in the sense that Bantustans were supposed to develop separately from the Republic of South Africa, in Palestine, we cannot ignore how Israeli policies produce walls of both space and time.[52] Julie Peteet notes that the policies of enclosure, including the wall of separation where *The Silent Minaret* concludes, produces a "denial of mutuality of time and space to Israelis and Palestinians."[53] Checkpoints produce their own timescapes of indefinite waiting; on Shukri's journey, he spent eight hours going through one building, and 12 hours travelling the 70 kilometers to Jerusalem.[54] In the occupied Palestinian territories, there are physical walls and barriers that produce separateness, but there are also paper walls of identity cards and permits. In M. Neelika Jayawardane's reading of the novel, Katinka's invitation to Kagiso to visit "is a reminder of their ongoing duty to others who are similarly trapped behind walls."[55] In dismantling the walls of time and space that might separate the dispossessed, the aesthetics of juxtaposition in

---

[49] Shukri, *The Silent Minaret*, 65.

[50] Shukri, *The Silent Minaret*, 65.

[51] Shukri, "Palestine Journey," 23.

[52] I am grateful to William Welty for pointing out that walls of space and time are also deployed in our own periodizations of literature (including contemporary literature). One way *The Silent Minaret* might comment on this tendency is through its deliberate flouting of these boundaries, showing us what we miss if contemporary literature is limited in its publication period, its preoccupations, or its national origins.

[53] Julie Peteet, "Closure's Temporality: The Cultural Politics of Time and Waiting," *The South Atlantic Quarterly* 117, no. 1 (January 2018): 45, https://doi.org/10.1215/00382876-4282037.

[54] Shukri, "Palestine Journey," 21.

[55] M. Neelika Jayawardane, "'Forget Maps': Documenting Global Apartheid and Creating Novel Cartographies in Ishtiyaq Shukri's *The Silent Minaret*," *Research in African Literatures* 45, no. 1 (2014): 18, https://doi.org/10.2979/reseafrilite.45.1.1.

The Silent Minaret thus gestures toward an ethical imperative that extends far beyond the novel's pages.

The link between the two geographies is represented explicitly in the chapter "Homelands," which uses an aesthetics of juxtaposition to reveal continuities between nationalist visions in South Africa and Israel. The chapter begins with Kagiso writing in his journal in Issa's abandoned room, and jumps to Katinka on the other side of the city, writing to her boyfriend Karim—a Palestinian national who has returned to the West Bank after his visa has expired. Shukri returns to Kagiso, who "returns to his journal to write, not like Katinka is doing, slowly, deliberately, letter by letter, but swiftly…" [56] The language of contemporaneous narrative—events happening at the same time, even if divided in space—is important to the novel's ethics of comparison and juxtaposition, insisting on a mutuality of time even if, for the moment, the mutuality of space is denied. The chapter's title, "Homelands," is one that resonates both with the Zionist vision of Israel and Bantustan policies alike; and yet, the novel also suggests that the dream of homelands animates, in a different way, the Palestinian demand for the right of return. Indeed, when Kagiso enters a bathroom in Brick Lane, he notices graffiti on the stall's walls, a chain that begins "Bangladesh used to be East Pakistan" and continues "Pakistan used to be India… Israel used to be Palestine/ Lebanon used to be Syria" and onward.[57] A parallel chain's predictions include, among others, "One day Basque will have been Spain…Palestine will have been Israel/ Chechnya will have been Russia." While Kagiso opts not to put his own homeland, Taung, on the list because he considers it "a now-settled dispute" that would be out of place "alongside so many contemporary and unresolved ones,"[58] the novel in fact questions the extent to which any of these disputes might be considered "settled" by showing the repetition and return of cycles of settler colonial dispossession.

Conclusion

In Katinka's observation that life in the West Bank is worse than the South African homelands, we see the work of comparison that accommodates both specificity and uniqueness. Juxtaposing South Africa and Palestine legitimizes the Palestinian liberation struggle, and highlights the "writing on the wall" of the eventual end of the occupation of Palestine. By bringing together these

---

[56] Shukri, *The Silent Minaret*, 37.

[57] Shukri, *The Silent Minaret*, 38.

[58] Shukri, *The Silent Minaret*, 38.

different times and places, Shukri additionally shows us not just similarities between human rights abuses and violations, but also the insidious work of empire to support tyrannical regimes everywhere. With *The Silent Minaret*'s expansive historical consciousness, produced through the powerful juxtaposition of the US, the UK, European settlement, South African apartheid, and finally, the occupied Palestinian territories, the work of comparison makes a compelling case to the novel's readers that we are all, still, implicated in empire and obligated to continue the struggle across both time and space.

The walls of space and time that we might erect in our own periodizations of cultural production—whether the operative concepts are post-45, post-89, postcolonial, post-apartheid, or post-9/11—threaten to occlude the salient features of the contemporary: the palimpsests of pasts both near and remote in the present, the entanglement of temporalities, and the way contemporary fiction troubles the present through juxtaposition, comparison, and analogy. This attention to form in the contemporary novel in English is one that Hyde and Wasserman promote in their analysis of the contemporary, noting that form "is never outside the messy histories that bring texts into the present," and that this present "is contingent upon specific pasts." [59] More than simply illuminating the imbrication of remote and recent pasts in the present, *The Silent Minaret* occupies the intersection between many of the "posts" that struggle to define the contemporary. Its postcolonial, post-apartheid passages echo later post-9/11 scenes from the global War on Terror, and its conclusion in Palestine implicitly calls forth the post-45 aftermath and, of course, the earlier British Mandate and the insidious, continued practice of settler colonialism to dispossess occupants in Gaza and the West Bank. Hyde and Wasserman open their essay with a reference to Giorgio Agamben's argument that "those who are contemporary are also untimely—they cannot fully coincide with their present."[60] Perhaps, then, Issa is a contemporary protagonist *par excellence*: a student of history who realizes that the past is no longer distinguishable from the now, whose disappearance registers his inability to be represented in the present. In this way, *The Silent Minaret* flouts expectations of the contemporary to announce breaks with the past, or exceptionalism, or newness; its use of juxtaposition underscores how patterns of oppression cycle across time and space as well. Though registering the untimeliness of our contemporary moment, the novel's message, I would argue, is undoubtedly timely after all.

---

[59] Hyde and Wasserman, "The Contemporary," 13-14.
[60] Hyde and Wasserman, "The Contemporary," 1.

Works cited

Anam, Nasia, Marina Bilbija, J. Daniel Elam, Arthur Rose, Amanda Lagji, Hadji Bakara, and Yogita Goyal. "Forms of the Global Anglophone." *Post45*, February 22, 2019. http://post45.org/sections/contemporaries/global-anglophone/.

Banita, Georgiana. *Plotting Justice: Narrative Ethics and Literary Culture after 9/11*. Lincoln: University of Nebraska Press, 2012.

Boehmer, Elleke. "Postcolonial Terrorist: The Example of Nelson Mandela." *Parallax* 11, no. 4 (August 2005): 46–55. https://doi.org/10.1080/1353464050 0331666.

De Loughry, Treasa. *The Global Novel and Capitalism in Crisis: Contemporary Literary Narratives*. New York: Palgrave Macmillan, 2020.

Falk, Richard. "International Law, Apartheid and Israeli Responses to BDS." In *Generation Palestine: Voices from the Boycott, Divestment and Sanctions Movement*, edited by Rich Wiles, 85-99. London: Pluto Press, 2013.

Ganguly, Debjani. *This Thing Called the World: The Contemporary Novel as Global Form*. Durham: Duke UP, 2016.

G siorek, Andrzej, and David James. "Introduction: Fiction Since 2000: Postmillennial Commitments." *Contemporary Literature* 53, no. 4 (Winter 2012): 609-627. https://www.jstor.org/stable/41819530.

Harvey, David. "Time-Space Compression and the Postmodern Condition." In *Modernity: Critical Concepts*, edited by Malcom Waters, IV, 98-118. London: Routledge, 1999.

Huehls, Mitchum. *Qualified Hope: A Postmodern Politics of Time*. Columbus: Ohio State UP, 2009.

Hyde, Emily, and Sarah Wasserman. "The Contemporary." *Literature Compass* 14, no. 9 (September 2017): 1-19. https://doi.org/10.1111/lic3.12411.

Jayawardane, M. Neelika. "'Forget Maps': Documenting Global Apartheid and Creating Novel Cartographies in Ishtiyaq Shukri's *The Silent Minaret*." *Research in African Literatures* 45, no. 1 (2014): 1-23. https://doi.org/10.2979/reseafrilite. 45.1.1.

Liao, Pei-Chen. *"Post"-9/11 South Asian Diasporic Fiction: Uncanny Terror*. New York: Palgrave Macmillan, 2013.

Martin, Theodore. *Contemporary Drift: Genre, Historicism, and the Problem of the Present*. New York: Columbia UP, 2017.

Peteet, Julie. "Closure's Temporality: The Cultural Politics of Time and Waiting." *The South Atlantic Quarterly* 117, no. 1 (January 2018): 43-64. https://doi.org/ 10.1215/00382876-4282037.

———. "The Work of Comparison: Israel/Palestine and Apartheid." *Anthropological Quarterly* 89, no. 1 (Winter 2016): 247-281. https://www.jstor.org/stable/43955521.

Pillay, Suren. "Checkpoints and Counterpoints: Edward Said and the Question of Apartheid." In *Apartheid Israel: The Politics of an Analogy*, edited by Jon Soske and Sean Jacobs, 108-114. Chicago: Haymarket Books, 2015.

Poyner, Jane. "Cosmopolitanism and Fictions of 'Terror': Zoë Wicomb's *David's Story* and Ishtiyaq Shukri's *The Silent Minaret*." *Safundi: The Journal of South African and American Studies* 12, no. 3-4 (2011): 313-330. https://doi.org/10. 1080/17533171.2011.586832.

Saint-Amour, Paul K. *Tense Future: Modernism, Total War, Encyclopedic Form.* Oxford: Oxford UP, 2015.

Shukri, Ishtiyaq. "Palestine Journey." In *Apartheid Israel The Politics of an Analogy,* edited by Sean Jacobs and Jon Soske, 19-28. Chicago: Haymarket Books, 2015.

———. *The Silent Minaret.* Johannesburg: Jacana, 2005.

Soske, Jon, and Sean Jacobs. "Apartheid/Hafrada: South Africa, Israel, and the Politics of Historical Comparison." In *Apartheid Israel: The Politics of an Analogy,* edited by Jon Soske and Sean Jacobs, 10-18. Chicago: Haymarket Books, 2015.

Theron, Cleo Beth. "Reconstructing the Past, Deconstructing the Other: Redefining Cultural Identity Through History and Memory in Ishtiyaq Shukri's *The Silent Minaret.*" *English Studies in Africa* 57, no. 2 (2014): 45-56. https://doi.org/10.1080/00138398.2014.963283.

Tutu, Desmond. "Foreword BDS." In *Generation Palestine: Voices from the Boycott, Divestment and Sanctions Movement,* edited by Rich Wiles, xii-xiv. London: Pluto Press, 2013.

Chapter 3

On the period currently known as Post45

Dan Malinowski

Rutgers University

Abstract

In her essay, "On the Period Formerly Known as the Contemporary," Amy Hungerford draws a line in the sand between earlier, non-rigorous scholarship on the literature of the second half of the 20th century, and a new group of scholars who turn away from mushy categories and to the hard facts of history. In practice, this entails a rejection of older Marxist periodizations of the contemporary. However, when the reason for this shift is described, it turns out that there is an ambiguity in Hungerford's own statement of this split.

In my essay, I argue that the distinction Hungerford makes is less one of method than of real political disagreement. What marks the shift between the new "acceptable" scholarship and the earlier work is a coded disagreement about what facts count for literary scholarship. Ultimately, I suggest that literary method often stands in the place of admitting real disagreement over the facts of the world, and acknowledging this both lays bare the stakes of our work as well as the role that our scholarship can serve.

Keywords: Hungerford, Amy; Contemporary Literature; Michaels, Walter Benn; Marxism; Post45 Group

***

In the poem "Tradition" by Juliana Spahr, from her collection of post-Occupy poems, *The Winter the Wolf Came*, the speaker attempts to reconcile the relationship between themselves and an other, a "not really me." [1] This relationship is defined by a giving: "I hold out my hand. / I hold out my hand. I hand over / and I pass on. Some call this mothering." [2] The poem explores the physical traces as well as the intangible cultures that we pass on, using the conceit of mothering to concretize the problem of environmental contamination and guilt that follows from our tradition: "Later I pass the breast cup to not

---

[1] Juliana Spahr, *That Winter the Wolf Came* (Oakland: Commune Editions, 2015), 53.

[2] Spahr, *That Winter the Wolf Came*, 53.

really me / a breast cup filled with sound insulation panels and imitation wood with a little nectar and sweetness / And not really me drinks it and then complains a little" about what is later described as "that cup of adhesives / that cup of fire retardants."[3] Tradition, in Spahr's poem and in the contemporary moment, designates not only the cultural models that we pass on, but the physical detritus of our lives—more and more, the past infects the present as a kind of physical accompaniment that is passed and passes on. These two aspects of tradition are not necessarily reducible to one another, but they certainly need to be considered together. However, at the same time, the poem's feeling is one of anxiety (some might call it paranoia) at the intangibles that are being passed on: the adhesives and fire retardants that permeate our lives accidentally, brought to us in complicated, technically-dense procedures both intended and not. Tradition, the poem tells us, is chemical as well as intellectual, accidental as well as intentional. Living in the world is almost too complicated to grasp in all its particulars and connections.

Building off of Spahr's insight, and the occasion of this collection, we can reread Amy Hungerford's field-defining essay, "On the Period Formerly Known as the Contemporary."[4] This essay allows us to think through some issues that continue to mark what I take to be the distinctive approach of Post45 as an academic group. Putting aside Twitter dustups that take it to task for a certain cliquishness, it is fair to think about what sort of political (or a-political) investments are forwarded by this founding essay, which, given the stature of its writer and the Post45 group for contemporary literary scholars, deserves a serious thinking-through.[5] In what follows, I will describe some of the theoretical commitments that Hungerford and Walter Benn Michaels subscribe to in order to account for how they see their work as a break with formerly dominant modes of periodizing the contemporary and to describe what I see as the important methodological mistake they make in defining this break as they do.

In her essay, Hungerford establishes a dichotomy that defines contemporary literature. Drawing from the work of Wendy Steiner, Hungerford argues that studies of the contemporary have often broken down in two ways: on the one hand, we have the "mainly white male authors" who are "literary" (Pynchon,

---

[3] Spahr, *That Winter the Wolf Came*, 54.

[4] Amy Hungerford, "On the Period Formerly Known as Contemporary," *American Literary History* 20, no. 1-2 (Spring-Summer 2008): 410-419, https://doi.org/10.1093/alh/ajm044.

[5] If there is a clique associated with Post45, it probably has more to do with the elitism and insularity of the programs at the top of the US News rankings, acknowledged or unacknowledged, than with anything else. And so thinking that there's a uniqueness to the operations of this one outlet strikes me as besides the point.

Barth, Gaddis, DeLillo), and, on the other, we have those who are sociological—a varied list that includes Morrison, Roth, Erdrich, Silko, Walker, and Didion.[6] She goes on to historicize this split, saying that the work of 90s literary critics was to end this divide, and, since, we have been working in a more pluralist field. This move, then, is further buttressed by Mark McGurl's work, which demonstrates how "the fiction of the postmodern white guys imagines itself finally in terms fully assimilable to the identitarian ethos of ethnic fiction" via the transformative processes of the creative writing classroom.[7]

In *Making Literature Now*, Hungerford expands on and models the sort of criticism she's arguing for in "On the Period." In the monograph, she points to the work of Bruno Latour as a lodestone for thinkers who want to get back to the concrete facts of life rather than mushy concepts of "the social."[8] For Hungerford, Latour demonstrates that "social connections only deserve the name when they are acted upon, that the social only exists at all when its networks are activated, and what's more, that social actors come in both human and non-human forms."[9] She goes on to give what has become a hallmark of Latour-influenced criticism, the list of nonhuman actors "books, apps, or delivery truck routs."[10] The reference to Latour here is crucial because it brings to the surface the methodological conservatism: empiricism. This allows Hungerford to dismiss "less" empirical positions, allowing us as scholars of the

---

[6] Hungerford, "On the Period Formerly Known as Contemporary," 411. We might add a third category here, prompted by the inclusion of Didion on this list—the writers who have been reclaimed by publishing as overwhelmingly significant in the opening of the twenty-first century. This list will include more white women (Didion, Sontag's fiction, Renata Adler, to list three names), though its racial diversity will remain unacceptable.

[7] Hungerford, "On the Period Formerly Known as Contemporary," 412-413.

[8] Amy Hungerford, *Making Literature Now* (Stanford: Stanford UP, 2016), 4.

[9] Hungerford, *Making Literature Now*, 4.

[10] Hungerford, *Making Literature Now*, 4. It's worth flagging that the impetus behind this turn is, at least in its framing, different for Latour than it is for Hungerford. Where Hungerford views Latour's thinking as a methodological innovation—shoring up the weak work of fuzzy and ill-defined terms by anchoring them in what we can identify empirically—Latour himself is much more interested in what his work will *do* in the world. As he points out in his famous intervention in critical inquiry, it's not that earlier forms of critique were wrong, which they may or may not be, but that their form encouraged a general rise in forms of suspicion. And here is where the Hungerford project diverges from the concurrent rise of surface reading or post-critique in the academy. This argument is not justified on anything other than academic grounds; the political effects of literary scholarship are, in this articulation, bracketed.

contemporary to move beyond "cultural materialist accounts of postmodernism that have been so powerful in defining the field."[11]

The attentive reader may notice an interesting sleight of hand in this dismissal. While Hungerford references Jameson's 1991 *Postmodernism, or the Cultural Logic of Late Capitalism*, the counter-example she actually explicates is Mark C. Taylor's *Confidence Games*. Hungerford writes, "Like Jameson in *Postmodernism*, Taylor locates the moment of postmodernism not in the fall of the Berlin Wall or at the close of the century, but on 16 August 1971, when global finance ceased to be tied to the gold standard, but this exacting historicism undermines itself the moment novels are invoked."[12] This is a confusing sentence to track. No one thinks that postmodernism begins with the Berlin Wall or at the close of the century, so why are these brought up as opposing dates that could potentially mark the start of the period? Second, and this is perhaps more important for a scholar so invested in empirical bona fides, Jameson never claims in the *Postmodernism* book that postmodernism begins in 1971, although he does argue that a swarm of crises in 1973 does constitute the signal, crystalizing event of the period.[13] She goes on to emphasize the weakness of Taylor's argument by dismissing his claim of a connection between William Gaddis's 1955 novel *The Recognitions* and Herman Melville's 1857 *The Confidence-Man*. For Hungerford, this suggests "that the literary embodiment of what [Taylor] defines as the condition of postmodernism cannot be neatly linked to genuinely transformative moments in the market. The connection works by analogy rather than by causation, which is why McGurl's more rigorously historical argument . . . seems to be more convincing."[14] So rigor means dismissing a date that no one in an argument seriously claimed, and then explaining the inappropriateness of trans-historical comparison.

What is at stake for Hungerford in terms of "rigor"? What do we learn from historical causality, and, specifically, a historical causality which, in all honesty, probably wouldn't pass muster in a more empirically-minded department? Moreover, how does critiquing Jameson via another critic's work tell us anything about his concept of the period of the postmodern? And finally, what, in the end, is gained by abandoning materialist accounts if, as Hungerford puts it, that

---

[11] Hungerford, "On the Period Formerly Known as the Contemporary," 413.

[12] Hungerford, "On the Period Formerly Known as the Contemporary," 413.

[13] Thanks to William Welty for pointing out that he does raise a specific date, if a different (and more diffuse) one than Hungerford accuses him of pinning the period on. For more, see Fredric Jameson, *Postmodernism or, The Cultural Logic of Late Capitalism* (Durham: Duke UP, 1991), xx-xxi.

[14] Hungerford, "On the Period Formerly Known as Contemporary," 413-414.

the "second half of the twentieth century sees not a departure from modernism's aesthetic but its triumph in the institution of the university and in literary culture more generally"?[15] Is this distinct from Jameson's contention that postmodernism is the complete modernization of the globe and its modes of production? It is difficult *not* to become a paranoid reader here: no reason has been given except for a self-evident incorrectness to the "cultural materialist" approach.[16] A debate over facts has once again been a fight over method.

Hungerford's interest in disturbing the received methods of the theoretically-inclined humanities has a long tradition in Americanist literary studies, and a particular tradition of doing so comes through the work and teaching of Hungerford's mentor, Walter Benn Michaels. Earlier in "On The Period," Hungerford flags her approval of the new canon for the contemporary that does not split between reportage and literary values. Thus, it is surprising to see her approvingly quoting Michaels, and happily summarizing his position: "The burden of his analysis is to argue that we mean what we say, that who we are has nothing to do with the meaning of what we say, and that to think of disagreement in terms of difference is to finally embrace the logic of both terrorism and biological essentialism."[17] This is also a not-inaccurate summary of how Michaels accounts for his own argument in *Shape of the Signifier*. There, he writes, "So the argument is, in miniature, that if you think the intention of the author is what counts, then you don't think the subject position of the reader matters, but if you don't think the intention of the author is what counts, then the subject position of the reader will be the only thing that matters."[18] This highlights an important philosophical underpinning of how a criticism based around causality and institutions will have to work: not only does the community and the things that one is taught matter, it becomes the ultimate and final ground for what a critic can reasonably say about the ideology of a work of art. By this I mean that, if I cannot say anything that I did not intend, then I can only say that which I have been historically and physically tied to. It seems to me that the earlier terms that Hungerford used (analogy and causality) essentially map on to Michaels's view that the two sides are either a reader's interpretation or the author's intent. The meanings of texts become determinate; the allegorical mode that much theory (and, specifically, Marxist theory) relies upon becomes unwelcome. Humorously, the intentionalist

---

[15] Hungerford, "On the Period Formerly Known as Contemporary," 418.

[16] A term used by Hungerford, but not by the Marxist interlocutors she's dismissing.

[17] Hungerford, "On the Period Formerly Known as Contemporary," 414.

[18] Walter Benn Michaels, *The Shape of the Signifier: 1967 to the End of History* (Princeton: Princeton UP, 2006), 12.

reading strategy indexes its own intentionalist roots—given the connection of a dissertation, Hungerford's training easily transfers to her views.

Looking at how Mark McGurl frames his project will show how this cashes out in newer histories of the discipline in more concrete terms. McGurl writes, in his introduction, "If I seem too willing to discount the enchantments of [creativity], and question the authority of [personal experience], it is only in the interest of restoring some balance in favor of the claims of collective life we live through institutions. Or rather . . . the collective life that institutions live through us."[19] This reference to the agency of institutions brings out an important aspect of this group's thought that is often overlooked in criticisms of Michaels's rhetoric. It is not the case that institutions or systems don't matter, but that it does not make sense to talk about some intangible, non-identifiable force (be it a racial, capitalist, or gendered unconscious) apart from the real institutions that enforce these things. And this helps to explain one of the earlier contradictions of this essay: how could a group that comes out of an intellectual tradition that dismisses difference as "biological essentialism" simultaneously view itself as a corrective to an earlier, racially homogenous view of literature? Well, it comes down to their interest in the classroom and criticism as an institution that has empirically identifiable habits. In short, the Post45 project may not be able to talk about what is called the psychic hold of slavery, but they can talk about how articles don't close read Toni Morrison for her aesthetics.

To sum up, what I am identifying as a dominant critical mood of Post45 (though it is not exclusive to post-45 or even twentieth-century literary studies), I want to argue that these critics rely on an intentionalist, causal structure that yields ways of understanding the present literary moment that may get us beyond the dumb distinctions between valued literary texts and texts for which the category of the literary does not apply. Second, I do want to recognize the power of their arguments. By focusing on the influence of the creative writing classroom, as in Mark McGurl's work, on the post-studio system in Hollywood, as in J. D. Connor's, and on the role of presses in the literary field, as in Lorin Stein's, we have been given a much stronger account of the roles that institutions play in determining artistic form. But, ultimately, the idea that this sort of work is a superior and more rigorous form of scholarship should be interrogated for the kind of subject that it assumes. And I, at least for my own purposes, do not think that this exhausts what we need to take into account in our discussions of works of art, and so I want to think about

---

[19] Mark McGurl, *The Program Era: Postwar Fiction and the Rise of Creative Writing* (Cambridge: Harvard UP, 2009), 21.

the mode of thought that Hungerford terms analogy, in order to rename it and to reconstruct its importance for literary studies and periodization.

Instead, we might say that this criticism proceeds not analogically, but with an eye towards totality. And as the product of a mediating procedure between the individual and the totality of their world, which at the same time creates that dialectical criticism helps us to understand how an individual comes to represent and reflect much more than their immediate circumstances. How can literary objects that precede a period reflect formal and thematic concerns of a later period, especially a later period that is associated with a particular date? With this in mind, it is worth thinking through the stakes of the dialectical subject as opposed to the intentionalist one described above by turning to Hegel. In Hegel's preface to the *Phenomenology of the Spirit,* he seeks to show how the Subject is created through movement and processes that precede and follow them as the context against which they are formed, and, since this knowledge comes about only through the movements of a diachronic system, the existence of a simple causal relationship between individual facts fails to account for the whole. He writes that knowledge can "only be expounded, as Science or system; and furthermore, that a so-called basic proposition or principle of philosophy, if true, is also false, just because it is only a principle."[20] That an individual fact can or cannot be applied at a given moment in the sequence of the system—like whether or not Taylor's reading of finance capital in *The Confidence-Man is* necessarily causally accurate—ignores how the world is not made up of atomistic propositions, but a continual process of negation and counter-negation that builds to the present moment. In short, identifying the logics of the present in the past isn't necessarily a problem—it is in fact, a boon, as it shows how history forms a real connection between texts and problems.[21]

---

[20] G. W. F. Hegel, *Phenomenology of Spirit,* trans. A. V. Miller (Oxford: Oxford UP, 1977), 13.

[21] We also have to recognize the selectiveness of intention: hundreds of years of literary history purport to speak for the real intentions of the text; the only difference is that in the late twentieth-century, critics admitted that they were making constructions that spoke for the past, rather than pretending to have access to the past itself. In light of this, the stakes of what the critic finds to be *intentional* becomes a co-creation. And if that's the case, then the critic, for better or worse, has a political choice to make when making these constructions: how, why, and for what purpose are our constructions useful? Of course, when we begin talking about the use of books the lines between different critical camps begin to blur—Felski and Jameson come together—but this, to me, only signals further what the real difference is. Namely, whether or not things like capital, race, or gender are valid questions for literary criticism (and literary work) in the first place.

If Hegel offers an explanation for how an individual's relationship to their social context works metaphysically, Marx, in his *Grundrisse*, concretizes this *Wissenschaftlich* type of thought by applying it to material production. He writes:

> In the succession of economic categories, as in any other historical, social science, it must not be forgotten that their subject—here, modern bourgeois society—is always a given, in the head as well as in reality, and that these categories therefore express the forms of being, the characteristics of existence, and often only individual sides of this specific society, this subject, and that therefore this society by no means begins only at the moment where one can speak of it as such; this holds for science as well.[22]

Marx is attacking the idea that the categories by which the contemporary moment operates can be taken as givens, that they are not part of a historical process "in the head as well as reality," as he put it. Moreover, the connections that one feels able to account for—like, say, a specific kind of causal relationship—are themselves historically contingent and only true in the specific analysis of the moment. But what of systems that may escape easily identifiable causal connections—such as the origin of finance capital, to bring us back to Hungerford's original provocation? The dialectic that Hegel outlines and Marx refines helps us to grasp just why texts that precede the contemporary can seem so of our moment, and, at the same time, help us understand why novelistic representations of the subject have, in their broadest strokes, remained pretty consistent over the past three centuries despite the drastic changes in social life.

Why does totality look like analogy? And has anyone considered this problem at length? Here, the work of Giovanni Arrighi is helpful: totality looks "like" other periods because business cycles are circular. As he writes, "Long periods of crisis, restructuring and reorganization, in short, of discontinuous change, have been far more typical of the history of the capitalist world-economy than those brief moments of generalized expansion along a definite developmental path like the one that occurred in the 1950s and 1960s."[23] Learning from

---

[22] Marx, Karl, *Grundrisse: Foundations of Political Economy*, trans. Martin Nicolaus (New York: Penguin Classics, 1993), 106.

[23] Giovanni Arrighi, *The Long Twentieth Century: Money, Power and the Origins of Our Times* (New York: Verso, 1994). In Arrighi's work, the analogy is one of the main tools of historical analysis, as it brings out the differences and similarities of historical periods. But rather than saying "this is like that," the bulk of Arrighi's (long) book is proving the similarities and differences between his four capitalist power-centers, while acknowledging

Arrighi, we see a model of historical thinking where historical exceptionality is, well, an exception, rather than a rule. That, in fact, capitalist history has proceeded similarly at ever-increasing scales, and to deny this fact is to miss how centers of power in the capitalist world have risen and fallen. But at the same time, we have to acknowledge that circularity, and similarity, must be treated cautiously—it's easy to fall into the trap of finding like-for-like. Scholars of the postwar period must be careful, then, to show their work. But Arrighi's work also helps us to see an implicit assumption in the framing of Post45, which is that it is, uniquely among latter-day developments in literary scholarship, devoted to a kind of American exceptionalism. To say that analogy is inappropriate comes to look a lot like a love of specificity that has real effects on the scale, scope, and influences on the projects that we produce as scholars.

What is the economically specific base for what we do? A problem for every scholar of literary (or cultural) phenomenon is that while it's easy to identify the conditions of possibility, it is nearly impossible to identify conditions of *im*possibility when it comes to matters of literary form or content—there are always going to be exceptions in the cultural field. But this isn't only the case for wide-ranging Marxist periodization—it is also, necessarily, the case for smaller and institutionally focused histories as well. Moreover, the fact that institutional histories, barring those that treat international organizations, are limited by having to, for reasons of human finitude rather than malice, focus on their instantiations in single countries. It is the case that Japanese and French literary establishments are producing vast amounts of books a year, in conditions that don't square neatly with anglophone narratives, such as the consolidation of the "big 5" publishing companies or the rise of MFA programs. Similarly, literary scholars don't often deal with the fact that the mid-list novels that make tenure-track careers do not keep the industry afloat nearly as much as the major genre categories or the latest expose of the current presidential administration.

The problem here isn't really one of method, but of priorities, and the issue is, as always, that some scholars wandered too far afield from the literary, and the past twenty years have been a retrenchment of small-c conservative scholarship while the world burned. Jacques Rancière's term for the politics of knowledge, the distribution of the sensible, clarifies the specifically territorial way in which facts can be included or excluded from communal knowledge: "This apportionment of parts and positions is based on a distribution of spaces,

---

that each has a similar arc. You could disagree with Arrighi's findings, and you could say that his mode of historical analysis is far too general. But in order to prove that he's wrong, you'd have to engage him on facts rather than method.

times, and forms of activity that determines the very manner in which something in common lends itself to participation and in what way various individuals have a part in this distribution."[24] For Rancière, the distribution of the sensible describes how and what forms of knowledge and inclusion are possible, with the ultimate goal of a broader, and more open play of politics among competing interests. What the rigor supposedly offered by Hungerford instead gives us is a shrunken distribution—one in which people who arbitrarily don't meet the level for inclusion in the conversation (whether as scholars, or, for the grad students of Columbia and Yale, laborers) can be safely excluded from consideration, thereby ensuring the survival of certain forms of knowledge over others. This is not to say that we should stick blindly to Jameson, Michaels, or whoever, but that words like "rigor" or "method" disguise the real debates that we're having as political subjects within the academy about the allowable scope of our work.

I want to conclude by broadening back out from the fight I've staged between analogy (or, now, dialectics) and causality. As I was preparing the original version of the presentation that led to this essay, I found that I was in the company of a critic whose recent work I've critiqued in this hotel in the past: Rita Felski, and her chapter entitled "Context Stinks."[25] Although I still disagree strongly that critique should play a less prominent role in the contemporary humanities, I think her description of the current state of historical analysis is accurate. She writes, "The backlash against [grand] historical narratives. . . has had less happy consequences: any form of cross-temporal thinking—tainted by guilt of association [with grand narratives]—has fallen out of favor. Instead, we are inculcated, in the name of history, into a remarkably static view of meaning, where texts are corralled amidst long-gone contexts and obsolete intertexts, incarcerated in the past, with no hope of parole."[26] I find in this diagnosis that Felski offers a kindred frustration with the limited way context has developed into hard forms of causality in Post45 and elsewhere. Although I couldn't care less for the Latourian solution that Felski offers, I think we're beginning to see analogy's comeback in literary studies. I just hope that it comes back in order to deal with the world in the totality of its messy histories. I would amend this title slightly: "Context Stinks, but nothing Is Not Context."

I want to conclude with another quote from Juliana Spahr's poetry that I think makes the point of my take much better than I can. She writes, "It might only

---

[24] Jacques Rancière, *The Politics of Aesthetics*, trans. Gabriel Rockhill (New York: Continuum, 2004), 12.

[25] [Editor's note] The presentation was for the 49th NeMLA Conference in Pittsburg, PA.

[26] Rita Felski, *The Limits of Critique* (Chicago: University of Chicago Press, 2015), 157.

be through the minor that we can feel enormity. It might be that there is nothing to epiphany if it does not hint at the moment of sweaty relation larger than the intimate. For what is epiphanic song if it doesn't spill out and over the many that are pulled from intimacies by oil's circulations."[27]

Works cited

Arrighi, Giovanni. *The Long Twentieth Century: Money, Power and the Origins of Our Times.* New York: Verso, 1994.

Felski, Rita. *The Limits of Critique.* Chicago: University of Chicago Press, 2015.

Hegel, G. W. F. *Phenomenology of Spirit.* Translated by A. V. Miller. Oxford: Oxford UP, 1977.

Hungerford, Amy. *Making Literature Now.* Stanford: Stanford UP, 2016.

———. "On the Period Formerly Known as Contemporary." *American Literary History* 20, no. 1–2 (Spring-Summer 2008): 410-419. https://doi.org/10.1093/alh/ajm044.

Jameson, Fredric. *Postmodernism or, The Cultural Logic of Late Capitalism.* Durham: Duke UP, 1991.

Marx, Karl. *Grundrisse: Foundations of Political Economy.* Translated by Martin Nicolaus. New York: Penguin Classics, 1993.

McGurl, Mark. *The Program Era: Postwar Fiction and the Rise of Creative Writing.* Cambridge: Harvard UP, 2009.

Michaels, Walter Benn. *The Shape of the Signifier: 1967 to the End of History.* Princeton: Princeton UP, 2006.

Rancière, Jacques. *The Politics of Aesthetics.* Translated by Gabriel Rockhill. New York: Continuum, 2004.

Spahr, Juliana. *That Winter the Wolf Came.* Oakland: Commune Editions, 2015.

---

[27] Spahr, *That Winter the Wolf Came,* 14.

Section II.
Towards a more global Post45

Chapter 4

"Workers of the world, unite!" Huck, Jim, and the Cold War's racial tensions

Daria Goncharova

The University of Kentucky

Abstract

With the onset of the Cold War and the rise of the civil rights movement in the U.S. and anti-colonial movements around the world, race became a cardinal point in the U.S.-Russia's competition for the friendship (and resources) of new nonwhite nations. Although post-45 scholars have done much to explore the intersection of U.S. foreign interests, social reforms, and cultural production in an American context, few have ventured beyond scratching the surface of Soviet antiracist and anti-American messaging. Following in the footsteps of Kate Baldwin and building on the work of such historians as Maxim Matusevich and Mary L. Dudziak, this article examines how Soviet filmmakers transformed the protagonists of *The Adventures of Huckleberry Finn* into a metaphor for interracial working-class alliance at the precise moment when Huck was being embraced as a quintessential American hero by American critics. By reading the Soviet film adaptation of Twain's novel, *Hopelessly Lost* (1973), against Cold War conceptualizations of race, material culture, and comradery, this essay renders visible the complex ways in which the Soviet Union held the United States accountable for their racial inequalities and imperialist tendencies, while simultaneously sacrificing specificity of local cultures and racial identities for the larger project of the overthrow of Western capitalism. Specifically, the changed ending in which Jim does not acquire freedom restages the racial conflict of *The Adventures of Huckleberry Finn* as an imperialist conflict between capitalist and communist blocs, while the film's drastic reduction of the novel's secondary characters and linguistic variety deprioritizes extensive examination of class distinctions in favor of anti-western critique. Focusing on questions of canonicity, race relations, and voice, this article not only challenges a United States-centered approach to American studies, but also offers new insight into the racial politics of the Cold War that continue to shape present-day relations between the United States and Russia.

Keywords: USSR; Cold War Literature; Twain, Mark; The Adventures of Huckleberry Finn; Cinema Studies

***

But Twain now—
in this war hysteria—
is no longer recognized
in contemporary America:
he has been cast from gloom and darkness
onto our shore,—
into our time!
— Nikolai Aseev "Mark Twain"[1]

When in 1949, Nikolai Aseev, an honored Soviet poet, dedicated an ode to his favorite writer, Mark Twain, he could hardly foresee just how prophetic his concluding lines would prove to be. In 1973, less than three decades after Aseev had metaphorically cast the renowned American writer onto the Soviet "shore," Mosfilm, the Soviet Union's leading film studio, released an adaptation of Twain's classic, *The Adventures of Huckleberry Finn*, titled *Sovsem Propashchij* (*Hopelessly Lost*).[2] Echoing Aseev's vision of Huck and Jim "stand[ing] / as brothers forever" under the "sun / spilling from the Volga to the Mississippi," Huck, played by a Russian child actor, and Jim, played by a Nigerian geology student at Moscow's Patrice Lumumba University, provided a visual symbol of the famous socialist slogan: "Workers of the world, unite!"[3] Instead of embracing Huck as "a morally idealized best American self" who chooses "going to hell" over betraying Jim, this Soviet adaptation—shaped by the Cold War tensions—presented Huck as a Soviet hero committed to Soviet vision of

---

[1] For the full poem in English translation, see J. M. Gogol, "Nikolai Aseev and Mark Twain," *Mark Twain Journal* 16, no. 4 (Summer 1973): 15-16.

[2] Although many of Twain's works were adapted to Soviet screen, *Hopelessly Lost* is the only one produced by Mosfilm, the Soviet Union's largest film studio that was known for producing feature films that would appeal to large segments of the population and could compete with foreign pictures. For comparison, Soviet film adaptations of Twain's *The Prince and the Pauper* in 1943 and 1972, *The Adventures of Tom Sawyer* in 1981, and *A Connecticut Yankee in King Arthur's Court* in 1988 were produced either by the smaller regional studios or by studios specializing in the production of children's films.

[3] Gogol, "Nikolai Aseev and Mark Twain," 16. It is worth noting that in the Soviet context, the Russian word *brat* (brother) is allusive to a comrade, a fellow socialist.

racial equality and the overthrow of capitalism.[4] By prioritizing Huck and Jim's struggle against the King and Duke over Huck's internal conflict and changing the story's ending to emphasize the relevance of this struggle to the contemporary moment, the film transforms Huck and Jim into a metaphor for interracial working-class alliance fighting against capitalist follies embodied by the pair of conmen on screen. Attending to the complexities, implications, and limitations of this transformation allows us to gain an insight into the racial politics of the Cold War that continue to shape the present-day relationship between the United States and Russia.

After World War II exposed the horrific effects of Nazi ideology and sparked anticolonial movements around the globe, "race became a strategic pawn" in the US-Russia competition for the friendship (and resources) of the new nonwhite nations.[5] With Soviet leaders never missing a chance to "highlight the hypocrisy of American racism amid U S. claims to leadership of the 'free world,'" the practice of racial segregation became "America's 'Achilles heel'" and a serious liability.[6] As historians have extensively demonstrated, America's interests abroad and the Cold War rivalry had a direct effect on the United States' domestic race relations, prompting a number of racial reforms in the 1950s and 1960s.[7] Yet, Mary L. Dudziak notes that although the civil rights' victories "helped bring an end to some of the most overt forms of segregation and discrimination, racial inequality remained."[8] With the onset of the Vietnam War that James E. Westheider argues showed "the United States exploit[ing] blacks in a racist war for a racist nation that offered little or nothing in return for their sacrifices," the Soviet Union continued to agitate for the worldwide people's liberation from Western racism and imperialism.[9]

Within this historical context, the scholarship on Twain in the 1940s-1970s acquired increasingly political and ideological undertones showcasing the

---

[4] Jonathan Arac, *Huckleberry Finn as Idol and Target: The Functions of Criticism in Our Time*, (Madison: University of Wisconsin Press, 1997), 9.

[5] Kate A. Baldwin, *Beyond the Color Line and the Iron Curtain: Reading Encounters between Black and Red, 1922-1963* (Durham: Duke UP, 2002), 180.

[6] Thomas Borstelmann, *The Cold War and the Color Line: American Race Relations in the Global Arena* (Cambridge: Harvard UP, 2001), 106; Mary L. Dudziak, *Cold War Civil Rights: Race and the Image of American Democracy* (Princeton: Princeton UP, 2011), 29.

[7] See, for example, Borstelmann, *The Cold War and the Color Line*; Dudziak, *Cold War Civil Rights*; Azza Salama Layton, *International Politics and Civil Rights Policies in the United States, 1941-1960* (Cambridge: Cambridge UP, 2000).

[8] Dudziak, *Cold War Civil Rights*, 248.

[9] James E. Westheider, *Fighting on Two Fronts: African Americans and the Vietnam War* (New York: New York UP, 1997), 3.

Cold War as a cultural rather than merely geopolitical warfare. Although Samuel Clemens has been perceived as "the founding father of the American literature" at least since William Dean Howells published *My Mark Twain* in 1910, it wasn't until the post-World War II years that *The Adventures of Huckleberry Finn* was established not only as an American masterpiece but also as America's moral compass, in a process that Jonathan Arac describes as "hypercanonization."[10] Influenced by the rhetoric of the Civil Rights Movement, "Cold War liberal American culture seemed to find in *Huckleberry Finn* a century-old solution to the race problems that had newly reemerged on the national agenda."[11] Thanks to the work of Lionel Trilling (1953), Henry Nash Smith (1958), and Walter Blair (1960), among many others, Huck, who chooses "going to hell" over betraying Jim, has come to represent a white savior, whose benevolence not only saves Jim but also allows the American reader to move past the nation's benighted past.[12]

While American scholars hailed both Mark Twain and his work as quintessentially American, Soviet criticism, which has been underway since Twain's work was first translated into Russian in 1874, promoted the image of Twain as the writer "whose spiritual homeland might well have been in Russia."[13] But if in pre-revolutionary Russia, Twain was generally framed either as a children's writer or as a humorist placed alongside such renowned Russian satirists as Nikolai Gogol, Anton Chekhov, and Mikhail Saltykov-Shchedrin, Soviet criticism, "with

---

[10] Neil Schmitz, "Mark Twain in the Twenty-First Century," *American Literary History* 16, no. 1 (March 2004): 122, https://doi.org/10.1093/ALH/AJH007.

[11] Arac, *Huckleberry Finn as Idol and Target*, 20.

[12] See Lionel Trilling, *The Liberal Imagination; Essays on Literature and Society.* (Garden City: Doubleday, 1953); Henry Nash Smith, *Introduction to Adventures of Huckleberry Finn* (Boston: Houghton Mifflin, 1958); and Walter Blair, *Mark Twain & Huck Finn* (Berkeley: University of California Press, 1962). For instance, Trilling describes Huck and Jim as a "community of saints" (107) and praises Huck's "moral sensitivity" (105).

[13] Joe B. Fulton, *Mark Twain Under Fire: Reception and Reputation, Criticism and Controversy, 1851-2015* (Rochester: Camden House, 2016), 100. Indeed, the speed with which Mark Twain rushed into Russian culture and the intensity with which his work was embraced in the Soviet Union are remarkable. *The Gilded Age: A Tale of Today* (1873) was translated in Russian in 1874; *The Adventures of Tom Sawyer* (1876) were serialized in 1877 and then published as a book in 1886; and *The Adventures of Huckleberry Finn* (1884) was serialized in 1885. For comparison, "Moby Dick (1851) was not translated into Russian until 1961" (xiii). Carl R. Proffer, *Soviet Criticism of American Literature in the Sixties; an Anthology.* (Ann Arbor: Ardis, 1972). For more on the publication and interpretation of the works by Mark Twain in pre-revolutionary Russia, see Ekaterina A. Stetsenko, "Mark Twain in Russian Periodicals. Part 1," *Studia Litterarum* 2, no. 2 (June 2017): 120-143, https://doi.org/10.22455/2500-4247-2017-2-2-120-143.

its marked proclivity for emphasizing social criticism and anti-imperialism," saw in Twain's novels a reflection of their own Anti-American sentiments.[14] In the post-World War II years, when American studies in Russia had just begun to transition from sporadic publications into an organized academic discipline, Twain was elevated to an American subversive who loved his country, but could not stand "позора, которым покрыли ее реакционеры-расисты и погромщики-линчеватели" (the shame which imperialists, robber-capitalists, the bribed reactionary ignorant rabble pogromist-lynchers have heaped on it).[15] Consequently, when *Hopelessly Lost* hit the screen, it joined the work of Soviet literary critics in reclaiming Twain as a socialist rather than as a national writer and Huck as an anti-imperialist rebel embodying the Soviet values of comradery and interracial solidarity.

Informed by these ideological tensions, the film was met with acclaim both from Soviet audiences and critics.[16] Soviet officials, in fact, were so impressed with Georgiy N. Daneliya's rendition of the famous novel that they insisted on the film's being entered into the 1974 Cannes Film Festival, replacing the already nominated *Mirror* by Andrei Tarkovsky, to demonstrate to the Western world that "Russians know *their* Twain."[17] The Cannes Festival, an international festival which that year alone attracted 2,000 film producers, critics, and distributors from around the globe, represented the perfect arena for Soviets and Americans to compete for the attention of the decolonizing and unaligned nations of Asia, Africa, and Latin America.[18] With the "Twain wars" mirroring the Cold War ideological divide, the film was meant to criticize Western vices embodied on screen by the King and Duke and to promote the image of international solidarity through a tender friendship between Huck and Jim.

---

[14] Fulton, *Mark Twain Under Fire*, 94-95. For the earlier reception of Twain, see Albert Parry, "Mark Twain in Russia," *Books Abroad* 15, no. 2 (Spring 1941): 168-175, https://doi.org.10.2307/40100322; Stetsenko, "Mark Twain in Russian Periodicals. Part 1."

[15] Abel Startsev (Абель Старцев), *Марк Твен и Америка [Mark Twain and America]* (Moscow: Pravda, 1980). For more on American studies, see Olga Antsyferova, "American Studies in Russia," *European Journal of American Studies* 1, no. 1 (January 2006): 1, https://doi.org/10.4000/ejas.366.

[16] Alexander Fedorov, *Cinema in the Mirror of the Soviet and Russian Film Criticism*, 2nd ed. (Moscow: ICO "Information for All," 2019), 32.

[17] For the quote, see Parry, "Mark Twain in Russia," 168, emphasis added. For Daneliya's reflection on the film, its reception, and its meaning, see Georgiy Daneliya (Георгий Данелия), *Безбилетный пассажир: Байки Кинорежиссёра [A Passenger Without a Ticket: Memoir]* (Moscow: Eksmo, 2006), 60.

[18] Vincent Canby, "New Cannes Festival Star: I. F. Stone," *The New York Times*, May 23, 1974, https://www.nytimes.com/1974/05/23/archives/new-cannes-festival-star-i-f-stone.html.

Yet, hindered by the paucity of the Soviet materials available to a foreign reader and diverted from a serious engagement with Red criticism by anti-communist sentiments, American critics largely overlooked *Hopelessly Lost* and, with it, Russian attempts to appropriate Huck and Twain to Soviet culture. Briefly mentioned in a few film adaptation studies of Mark Twain and virtually ignored by American literary critics, *Hopelessly Lost* has, ironically, lived up to its title.[19] A handful of American scholars from the 1940s-1970s who do attempt to engage with Soviet criticism either focus solely on the reception of twentieth-century American authors or merely scratch the surface of Twain studies in Russia without putting them into the Cold War context.[20] Although since the 1970s, scholars have developed new interpretations of the text, the hypercanonization of *The Adventures of Huckleberry Finn* and the rhetoric of American exceptionalism continue to haunt American studies as Twain is upheld as "the leading translator of who and what the 'American' was and, to a large extent, still is."[21] By turning scholarly attention to this overlooked Soviet adaptation of Twain's *Huckleberry Finn*, this essay joins the work of Kate Baldwin, Donald E. Pease, and other Cold War scholars who engage with transnational cultural analysis to deconstruct and complicate the binaries of the Cold War. Specifically, by breaking down the conflict in *Hopelessly Lost*, this essay renders visible the complex ways in which the Soviet Union held the United States accountable for their racial inequalities and imperialist tendencies,

---

[19] See Perry Frank, "Adventures of Huckleberry Finn on Film," in *Huck Finn among the Critics: A Centennial Selection*, ed. Thomas M. Inge (Frederick: University Publications of America, 1985), 293-313; Clyde V. Haupt, *Huckleberry Finn on Film: Film and Television Adaptations of Mark Twain's Novel, 1920-1993* (Jefferson: McFarland, 1994); Kate Newell, "'You don't know about me without you have read a book:' Authenticity in Adaptations of 'Adventures of Huckleberry Finn,'" *Literature/Film Quarterly* 41, no. 4 (October 2013): 303-316.

[20] See Proffer, *Soviet Criticism of American Literature in the Sixties; an Anthology*. Proffer focuses exclusively on Soviet reception and responses to the twentieth-century American authors, while confining Twain and other popular nineteenth-century writers to footnotes. Although admitting Twain's popularity in the USSR, both Albert Parry and Maurice Friedberg dismiss Soviet criticism on the grounds of "misunderstanding" Twain or marketing him as a "children's writer." See Parry, *Mark Twain in Russia*, 169; Maurice Friedberg, "The U.S. in the U.S.S.R.: American Literature through the Filter of Recent Soviet Publishing and Criticism," *Critical Inquiry* 2, no. 3 (Spring 1976): 531, https://doi.org/10.1086/447854.

[21] For the quote, see Shelley Fisher Fishkin, *Lighting out for the Territory: Reflections on Mark Twain and American Culture* (Oxford: Oxford UP, 1998), 8. For the discussion of American studies' roots in the Cold War and the framework of American exceptionalism, see Donald E. Pease, *The New American Exceptionalism* (Minneapolis: University of Minnesota Press, 2009), 8-13.

while simultaneously sacrificing the specificity of local cultures and racial identities for the larger project of the overthrow of Western capitalism.

Black skin, white voice, and Russian *Izba*

Because antiracism messaging helped Soviets "to distinguish [their] own 'socialist virtues' from the evils of 'capitalist' race discrimination," propaganda campaigns against Western racism were an important part of the Soviets' cultural warfare toolkit from the formation of the USSR until its collapse.[22] Recognizing the appeal that "the denunciation of capitalism and the promise of a socialist utopia" held for historically discriminated and economically disadvantaged racial and ethnic groups around the world, the Soviet Union, with the onset of the Cold War, focused on publicly condemning American lynching, segregation, and other forms of racial violence, not only professing the moral superiority of the Soviet people but also establishing the socialist system as a condition of racial harmony.[23] Yet, as historian Maxim Matusevich recently observed, "the Soviet Union's engagement with race was hardly unproblematic."[24] In an attempt to streamline racial equality and appeal both to African Americans and emerging independent African nations, the Soviet vision of internationalism in the 1950s-1960s "assumed the form of a racial paternalism" that "subordinated African Americans and other [ethnic] groups to Russians as the 'first among equals.'"[25] With the state maintaining that "progress toward socialism could only come in the national form—infused, as the saying went, with socialist content," the Soviet promise of an equalizing

---

[22] Barbara Keys, "An African-American Worker in Stalin's Soviet Union: Race and the Soviet Experiment in International Perspective," *The Historian (Kingston)* 71, no. 1 (Spring 2009): 34, https://www.jstor.org/stable/24454160. For an overview of historical shifts in Soviet antiracist rhetoric and foreign policies, see Maxim Matusevich, "Soviet Anti-Racism and Its Discontents: The Cold War Years," in *Alternative Globalizations: Eastern Europe and the Postcolonial World*, eds. James Mark, Artemy M. Kalinovsky, and Steffi Marung (Bloomington: Indiana UP, 2020), 229-250. On the Soviet relationship with African Americans and African nations, see Baldwin, *Beyond the Color Line and the Iron Curtain*; Joy Gleason Carew, *Blacks, Reds, and Russians: Sojourners in Search of the Soviet Promise* (New Brunswick: Rutgers UP, 2008); Maxim Matusevich, "An Exotic Subversive: Africa, Africans and the Soviet Everyday," *Race & Class* 49, no. 4 (April 2008): 57-81, https://doi.org/10.1177/0306396808089288.

[23] Jeff R. Woods, *Black Struggle, Red Scare: Segregation and Anti-Communism in the South, 1948--1968* (Baton Rouge: Louisiana State UP, 2003), 21.

[24] Matusevich, "Soviet Anti-Racism and Its Discontents," 229.

[25] Meredith L. Roman, *Opposing Jim Crow: African Americans and the Soviet Indictment of U.S. Racism, 1928-1937* (Lincoln: University of Nebraska Press, 2012), 105.

utopia hinged on the substitution of racial hierarchies with the hierarchy of nations and the suppression of racial and ethnic identities. [26]

Grounded in these ideals of "colorblind internationalism and proletarian solidarity," *Hopelessly Lost* reflects the complex and, at times, contradictory interplay between Soviet aspirations for racial equality and Soviet racializing practices.[27] Committed to anti-Western critique, the film prioritizes scenes that draw attention to the social ills that, in the Soviet interpretation, constituted the foundation of a capitalist regime: racial exploitation and mindless pursuit of wealth. Since American racism is undermined through the growing rapport between Huck (Roman Madyanov) and Jim (Feliks Imokuede), while capitalist greed is condemned through the satirization of the King (Yevgeny Leonov) and Duke (Vakhtang Kikabidze), the film centers on these four characters. By shrinking Twain's array of characters to these four, the film rejects the novel's extensive examination of class distinctions in favor of the oversimplified dichotomy between "the authenticity and closeness of Huck and Jim" and "the fraudulent claims of superiority by the King and Duke" that is then imposed over the Cold War binary oppositions between a socialist way of life and capitalist abuses, interracial solidarity and racism.[28] Specifically, the film's first

---

[26] Eric D. Weitz, "Racial Politics without the Concept of Race: Reevaluating Soviet Ethnic and National Purges," *Slavic Review* 61, no. 1 (Spring 2002): 10, https://doi.org/10.2307/2696978. For more on Soviet construction of race, ethnicity, and nationality, see Keys, "An African-American Worker in Stalin's Soviet Union;" Alaina Lemon, "The Matter of Race," in *Ideologies of Race: Imperial Russia and the Soviet Union in Global Context*, ed. David Rainbow (Montreal: McGill-Queen's UP, 2019), 59-76; Weitz, "Racial Politics without the Concept of Race." As Keys points out, Soviet Union's claim to be free of American-like racism was partly true because "Soviet ethnic and national categorizations did not align with the racialized thinking that prevailed in the United States and Western Europe" (37). But since the Soviet Union's hierarchy of nations relied on the simultaneous suppression and reinforcement of certain elements of ethnic and racial hierarchies, the Soviet Union was not free from the discrimination against and persecution of Jews, Muslims, and Caucasian ethnic groups such as Chechens, Ingush, and Tatars. For an overview of Soviet ethnic purges, see Ian Law, *Red Racisms: Racism in Communist and Post-Communist Contexts* (New York: Springer, 2016), 1-36.

[27] Matusevich, "Soviet Anti-Racism and Its Discontents," 229.

[28] Arac, *Huckleberry Finn as Idol and Target*, 106. Although the first and second acts of *Hopelessly Lost* closely follow the plot of Twain's novel, the supporting characters such as Huck's Pap, Widow Douglas, Miss Watson, and Buck are given much less screen time in order to prioritize the development of Huck and Jim's relationship. For instance, a feud between the Grangerfords and Shepherdsons is reduced to a one-minute segment during which Huck meets Buck in the field, learns about the meaning of a feud, and then witnesses Buck getting shot. Huck never reflects on this experience, and these events are never brought up again in the film.

act focuses largely on the developing relationship between Huck and Jim, while the film's second and third acts complete the duo's transformation into a metaphor for communist interracial alliance by contrasting them with the "royals." But, because by the time the King and Duke enter the scene, the viewer must already perceive Huck and Jim as more Soviet than American, the film's introduction has to resolve an ideological paradox: it has to "Sovietize" both Jim and Huck, while simultaneously "othering" Jim to establish racial discrimination as the part of American "civilized society."

Nothing exemplifies these contradictory imperatives better than the scene with a magic hairball that introduces Jim to the viewer. As the film cuts abruptly from the opening dinner sequence at Miss Watson's house to the magic hairball scene, a close-up of Huck's white face brightly lit by the dining room lights is instantaneously substituted with a close-up of Jim's face that appears even darker in the evening shadows stretching across the slave cabin's wall behind him. This jump cut emphasizes the "exotic otherness" of Jim, for the facial features of Feliks Imokuede, a Nigerian exchange student, contrast with the pale skin, light hair, and blue eyes of Roman Madyanov, a Russian child actor. But as the camera slowly pulls back to reveal Huck sitting next to Jim at the doorstep of his cabin, Jim begins speaking the clearest Russian devoid of any accent. Fearing that Imokuede's strong Nigerian accent would render Jim's part incomprehensible to a Soviet viewer and, thus, would detract from the film's message, Daneliya decided that Imokuede's performance had to be dubbed. In fact, the speech of all actors in *Hopelessly Lost* is devoid of any dialectical patterns and instead follows the rules of standard Russian, for Daneliya chose against trying to replicate the linguistic variety of Twain's novel, claiming that "the result would have been very artificial and would not have brought us closer to the spirit of the novel."[29]

The achieved result, however, is rather uncanny, because, in many close-ups, the Russian speech dubbed over Imokuede's dialogue does not match the actor's lip movements.[30] This mismatch brings to mind Slavoj Žižek's claim that voice carves a hole in an image as it attempts to fill it with meaning.[31] With

---

[29] Theodore Shabad, "'Huck Finn' Put on Film in Soviet," *The New York Times*, November 29, 1972, https://www.nytimes.com/1972/11/29/archives/huck-finn-put-on-film-in-soviet.html.

[30] New to Russia and its language, Imokuede, reportedly, spoke "a Nigerian-accented mixture of English and Russian" on set, which must have made the dubbing process even more technically challenging. See Shabad, "'Huck Finn' Put on Film in Soviet."

[31] Although Žižek's argument focuses mainly on Lacanian theory and the relationship between voice, subjectivity, and reality, his point that voice "points toward a gap in the field of the visible, toward the dimension of what eludes our gaze" is relevant for the discussion of sound and dubbing in film. See Slavoj Žižek, "I Hear You With My Eyes," in

Daneliya's Jim looking nothing like a Russian of Slavic descent, but sounding exactly like one, these moments of audiovisual asynchrony draw attention to "holes" in the Soviet conceptualization of race. A geology student at Moscow's University, Imokuede was chosen for the part not because of his acting skills but because his pronounced facial features corresponded to a Soviet idea of what a Black slave should look like. Nevertheless, while the camera work sensationalizes visual signs of racial difference, the sound work repudiates their validity. Unlike Twain's Jim, whose "Missouri Negro dialect" betrays his lack of education and his low social status, Daneliya's Jim, thanks to the miracles of dubbing, speaks the same clear Russian that comes from the mouths of other characters, thus erasing any linguistic variations between upper-class and low-class characters and bringing into question the entire social hierarchy of American society. On the surface, this homogenization shifts the dynamics of power by severing the "natural" link between a Black body and a Black voice and evoking Frantz Fanon's postulate that "to speak a language is to appropriate its world and culture." [32] However, the forced nature of this linguistic standardization—the complete erasure of the Black voice and the substitution of all regional dialects with standard Russian—speaks to the hypocrisy of a Soviet vision of internationalism. Evoking Soviet policies of forced assimilation, Imokuede's dubbed speech points to a Soviet tendency to hide "Russian domination and imperial domination behind internationalist rhetoric." [33]

Because in the film the issue of translation includes not only "what is being translated onto film," but also "how viewers translate among different sign-systems they are seeing on a screen," the misalignment of Jim's ethnic and linguistic identity must be read against other sites of "Russification" brought by the new elements of the mise-en-scène. [34] Filmed almost entirely on location— mainly the Dnieper river and the Baltic region— *Hopelessly Lost* uses local buildings and spaces that, to Daneliya, "evoked towns along the Mississippi." [35] Consequently, Jim's slave cabin looks surprisingly similar to a peasant's *izba*

Gaze and Voice as Love Objects, eds. Renata Salecl and Slavoj Žižek (Durham: Duke UP, 1996), 93. For the more nuanced discussion of the issues specific to the cinematic voice and dubbing practices, see Tom Whittaker and Sarah Wright, *Locating the Voice in Film: Critical Approaches and Global Practices* (Oxford: Oxford UP, 2016).

[32] Frantz Fanon, *Black Skin, White Masks* (New York: Grove Press, 2008), 21.

[33] For the quote, see Law, *Red Racisms*, 19. For Law's comments on the Soviet Union's forced assimilation of Tatars, Jews, and Roma, see Law, *Red Racisms*, 5, 13-14, and 22, respectively.

[34] Michael Wood, "The Languages of Cinema," in *Nation, Language, and the Ethics of Translation*, eds. Sandra Bermann and Michael Wood (Princeton: Princeton UP, 2005), 79.

[35] Shabad, "'Huck Finn' Put on Film in Soviet."

(hut), a one-story log house that even in the 1970s was still fairly common in rural areas of Soviet Russia. Although nowadays it is impossible to verify if the building that we see on screen is in fact an old peasant's hut or a prop constructed for the film, the point is that, from the perspective of the Soviet viewer, it could be either, for it would evoke the realities of the Russian countryside.

In a further appeal to the audience's emotions, the film introduces two additional characters: Jim's wife and his daughter, Elizabeth. Although the two appear on screen for no longer than ten seconds, their film debut is critical for completing both Jim's humanization and "Sovietization." As Jim attempts to see into Huck's future with the help of the magic hairball, the camera pans to the right to reveal Jim's wife and daughter approaching from the river, carrying what looks like a heavy basket of freshly washed laundry. Since, "by the late 1980s, only half of all houses in [the Russian] countryside had running water," rural women were used to washing laundry by hand in the river or in the washtub, making this depiction of African American life feel like a familiar sight to a Soviet viewer.[36] By evoking the familiar elements of Russian rural life to comment on the hardships of African American slaves, *Hopelessly Lost* emphasizes the "cross-racial affinity between Russians and blacks as marginalized, world historical 'others.'"[37] Although serfdom in tsarist Russia and later social stratification in the Soviet Union were never racially motivated in the same way that slavery in the United States was, the mise-en-scène suggests that African Americans and Soviet people share a similar history of marginalization.

By contrast, Huck, dressed in a crispy white shirt, an expensive-looking black suit, and shiny black shoes, appears closer to the genteel American society than to Jim, and, by extension, an average Soviet viewer. In addition, as Huck gets up to leave, his dialogue betrays the traces of Western racial thinking that the film sets off to condemn: "Джим, ты вот что, не говори никому что я тут с тобой. А тот скажут совсем пропащий Гек—с неграми компанию водит" [Listen, Jim, don't tell anyone that I was here with you. Otherwise, they'd say that Huck must be hopelessly lost—to associate with Negroes].[38] These lines, however, are crucial in introducing the viewer to the main message of the film contained in its title—that the state of "being hopelessly lost" is determined by how the person orients himself in relation to the society's dominant norms and values.

---

[36] Liubov Denisova and Irina Mukhina, *Rural Women in the Soviet Union and Post-Soviet Russia*, (London: Routledge, 2010), 153.

[37] Baldwin, *Beyond the Color Line and the Iron Curtain*, 2.

[38] Georgiy Daneliya (Данелия, Георгий), *Hopelessly Lost*, Mosfilm Studios, 1973. Unless otherwise noted, all translations are my own.

By having Huck early on in the film express fear of social repercussions and ostracization for his friendship with Jim, Daneliya establishes that the white American society in which Huck finds himself is predicated on discrimination and subjugation of Black people. Yet, Huck's linguistic choices make clear— even as he voices his concerns about the public opinion—that he does not align himself with the society's norms. By using the abstract "they" and referring to himself in the third person, Huck creates a gap between his real self and the persona that the society wants him to adopt.

These linguistic choices along with the use of the voiceover allow the Soviet viewer to identify with the young protagonist and perceive him as a fellow comrade from the very beginning, while simultaneously holding "them"— white American society—accountable for their racism. Consequently, the irony of the film's title lies in the fact that, in the Soviet interpretation, Huck is hopelessly lost only as long as he abides by the norms and values of the American "lost" society. This playful pun also helps the viewer to overlook the biggest irony of all—that, with a Russian actor's voicing over of a Nigerian student playing an African American slave in the Soviet production of Twain's novel, *Hopelessly Lost* relies on the simultaneous repudiation and reinforcement of racial difference while presenting itself as an anti-racist film.

The Soviet way of life—uncorrupted by capitalist greed

In 1972, the Communist Party issued a decree instructing the USSR State Committee for Cinematography, a.k.a Goskino USSR, "to raise the ideological and creative level of film" to counteract their enemies' efforts to demoralize the Soviet public.[39] Called upon to assert the Soviet Union's superiority just as the economy began to show the first signs of stagnation, the Soviet film industry cultivated the idea that the "socialist way of life" was superior to Western capitalism because it endowed Soviet people with moral virtues rather than with financial gains. In the words of the Soviet historian Christine Evans, "The concept of the 'socialist way of life' allowed the Soviet Communist Party to

---

[39] Paula A. Michaels, "Navigating Treacherous Waters: Soviet Satire, National Identity, and Georgii Daneliia's Films of the 1970s," *Historical Journal of Film, Radio, and Television* 29, no. 3 (2009): 346, https://doi.org/10.1080/01439680903145587. With the end of the Khrushchev Thaw in the mid-1960s, the Soviet state revived many practices of Stalinist-era cinema and censorship to prevent the seeds of Western influence from taking root. For the discussion of Soviet cinema and the film industry during and after the Thaw, see Valery Semenovich Golovskoy, *Behind the Soviet Screen: The Motion-Picture Industry in the USSR, 1972-1982* (Ann Arbor: Ardis, 1986); Tony Shaw and Denise Jeanne Youngblood, *Cinematic Cold War: The American and Soviet Struggle for Hearts and Minds* (Lawrence: UP of Kansas, 2014), 159-167.

refocus its competition with the West not on material conditions and standards of living, but on qualities that were far more difficult to measure directly—morals, values, and emotional, interpersonal, or ethical 'atmospheres.'"[40]

In this context, Daneliya's rendition of the King and Duke's financial schemes acquires strong anti-Western undertones, for the conmen's obsession with money and their readiness to lie for it exemplify the Soviet postulate that the capitalist pursuit of wealth leads to one's moral decay.[41] Consequently, in contrast to American film adaptations of *The Adventures of Huckleberry Finn* that treat the King and Duke mainly as a comic relief, the Soviet production turns the two into major antagonists.[42] The King is portrayed as an ignorant and violent alcoholic who can fake eloquence only when there is money on the line, while the Duke is presented as a misunderstood artist whose genteel aspirations eventually lead him to a downfall. Together, they represent two evils of "lost" American culture as defined by Soviet standards, dehumanizing capitalism and bourgeois demagoguery, warning the Soviet viewer against potential infatuation with the exploitative individualist culture of the West.

With this shift in the film's focus—from Huck's internal conflict to Huck and Jim's active opposition to the King and Duke—*Hopelessly Lost* develops those scenes in which the conmen take advantage of the pair and cheat them out of the money that Huck and Jim need in order to obtain a ticket for the steamboat to Cairo. For instance, when rehearsing the balcony scene from *Romeo and Juliet*, the Duke tasks Huck with reading for Juliet's Nurse and makes Jim construct the props for their play and imitate the birds' singing at his signal.[43] Although the King and Duke largely dismiss or belittle Jim's contribution, the camera work draws the audience's attention to the amount of work Jim puts in the play's production. Specifically, the King and Duke's theatrical debut opens with a close-up shot of Jim pulling up a cardboard cutout of the moon as he whistles to create the illusion of birds' singing. His physical efforts and concentrated face are then contrasted with the King and Duke's bored

---

[40] Christine Evans, "The 'Soviet Way of Life' as a Way of Feeling. Emotion and Influence on Soviet Central Television in the Brezhnev Era," *Cahiers Du Monde Russe* 56, no. 2-3 (April 2015): 544, https://doi.org/10.4000/monderusse.8201.

[41] Although it would be a stretch to call the King and Duke "capitalists" in the modern sense of the word, the binary thinking of the Cold War that maintained oppositions between communism and capitalism, East and West, good and bad, would make a Soviet viewer see the duo as the metaphor for capitalism.

[42] Frank, "Adventures of Huckleberry Finn on Film," 299.

[43] *Hopelessly Lost*, 49:50-50:10.

expressions and slouching poses as the wide shot of the stage reveals an empty theater.[44]

Expecting to get a fair share for their efforts, Huck and Jim are shown to work hard for the King and Duke; yet, they receive nothing, an outcome that Daneliya underscores by developing the scene in which the conmen count their loot.[45] As the camera focuses on the pile of bills and coins shining on the King's lap in the dim light of the raft's fire, the King proudly announces that they earned $440 and that he intends to split the money equally between him and the Duke—$220 for each. The latter, being in a good mood after getting away with his scheme, fishes out a coin from his pocket and tosses it to Jim as he remarks that they actually made $441. The camera focuses on Huck and Jim, staring at the coin in excitement and surprise, as Jim bites down on it to see if it is real. But the King quickly snatches it away from him, making Huck point out that they were promised an equal share: "Нам ведь тоже полагается—ну вы же обещали" [What about us—come on, you promised].[46] In response, the King states that "деньги портят детей" [money spoils children], ignoring the multiple pronoun "we/us" in Huck's protest.[47] In the context of "Soviet way of life" ideology, Huck's plea for equal distribution of income between each "worker" establishes him as a proper Soviet citizen of high moral standards. In contrast, the King is depicted as greedy, immoral, and therefore anti-Soviet because he takes advantage of Huck's trust and dismisses Jim's claim for an equal share on the grounds that, as a slave, he is not entitled to any payment for his labor.[48]

With Jim presented as a victim of capitalist injustice, the film also suggests that racialized violence is an evitable byproduct of the capitalist system that pits bourgeoisie against proletariat, workers against workers, and race against race. From the first scene of their interaction, the King and Duke are depicted as a serious (and physical) threat to both Huck and Jim's interracial utopia. For instance, before the invaders of the raft even introduce themselves, the King

---

[44] *Hopelessly Lost*, 50:45-51:05.

[45] *Hopelessly Lost*, 56:07-57:37.

[46] *Hopelessly Lost*, 57:02-57:07.

[47] *Hopelessly Lost*, 57:09.

[48] For comparison, the original scene in *Huckleberry Finn* shows the King and Duke dividing the sum of $465 in between themselves, with Huck and Jim disapproving of these "reglar rapscallions" and other royals but not laying a claim to the money. See Mark Twain, *The Adventures of Huckleberry Finn* (New York: Harper & Bros., 1912), 212. By making the above changes to draw attention to the King and Duke's exploitation of Jim, *Hopelessly Lost* foregoes fidelity to the text in favor of socialist critique of profit-seeking enterprises

gives Huck a slap on the head for staring and then kicks Jim, suspecting that he must be a runaway slave. The most violent episode of the film, however, comes at the end of the second act when, after barely escaping punishment for deceiving the Wilks sisters, the King takes his anger out on Huck and Jim. Blaming Huck for their plan's failure, the King knocks Huck down on his back, and when Jim intervenes, threatens the latter with an ax. Surprisingly graphic, this scene not only exposes the King's greed as a fueling force behind his racist and aggressive tendencies, but also reaffirms the image of Huck and Jim as comrades standing shoulder to shoulder against the Western follies embodied by the King. In contrast to the earlier American adaptations, which are often chastised for presenting Jim as passive or submissive, Daneliya's Jim openly confronts the white man as he tells the King, "не троньте мальчишку" [Don't you touch the boy].[49] This defiance on the part of the slave causes the still-panting King to stop dead in his tracks. As he lifts up his head in disbelief uttering, "Что ты сказал?" [What did you say?], the medium shot shows him glancing around the raft in search of a weapon before his eyes land on an ax next to him.[50] The film cuts to a close-up of the ax swinging into the air, and in the next shot, the King lunges forward yelling, "Убью! Раб!" [I'll kill you! Slave!].[51] But Huck quickly jumps in front of Jim screaming at the top of his lungs, "Не убивайте его! Это мой негр!" [Don't kill him! This is my Negro!].[52] Although Huck's speech evokes the mentality of white masters, his body language—his body pressing against Jim's stomach as he tries to shield him from an ax—makes it clear that the reference to Jim as property is meant for the King, who measures the world around him in terms of profit and loss. Hence, somewhat paradoxically, Huck has to refer to Jim as a possession and underscore the monetary value of his body in order to save his life. The viewer, however, knows by this point that Huck's appropriation of racist discourse is just a performance, a tactic, showcasing his code-switching skills, for the introduction of the King and Duke to the raft clearly marks a new stage in Huck and Jim's relationship.

While in earlier scenes Huck is shown to doubt his decision to help a runaway slave, his concerns about what others might think disappear when the two conmen come to pose as an active threat to Jim's well-being. The first night that the four share the raft, Huck and Jim are shown to have a heart-to-heart conversation by the fire, while the King and Duke snore away in drunken

---

49 *Hopelessly Lost*, 1:18:57.

50 *Hopelessly Lost*, 1:19:01.

51 *Hopelessly Lost*, 1:19:05.

52 *Hopelessly Lost*, 1:19:06-1:19:08.

slumber. While the night setting evokes the scene with the magic hairball, also filmed at night, the lighting and composition of the shot offers a striking contrast to Huck and Jim's first scene together. Although in both scenes Huck and Jim are shown sitting side by side, the bright light of the slave cabin emphasizes the social (and physical) gap between the two as it illuminates the cabin's run-down walls, Huck's elegant attire, Jim's shabby clothes, and the empty space between the two. In contrast, the dimly lit scene on the raft drowns everything around them in blackness so that only their faces are illuminated by the fire. In a close-up shot, Huck and Jim's faces appear only inches away from each other, with the flickering light of the fire dancing against the white and black skin, at times enhancing and at times nearly eliminating the signs of racial difference, as it casts dark shadows on Huck's tanned body. With the dancing light bringing the very stability of racial categories in question, the scene's underlying message is that, with no material objects in sight to signal Huck and Jim's social status, their "inner" similarities (their morals and values) outweigh their "outer" differences (their skin color).

As the mise-en-scène nearly eliminates their racial differences, Huck and Jim's dialogue foregrounds their shared goodness and establishes Huck's commitment to equality as the reason behind his decision to help Jim. After weighing their options, Huck concludes that staying with the two conmen is safer than trying to get through the Southern territory on their own: "Джим, ничего не поделаешь. На берег не сунешься. Здесь юг. Тебя сразу же линчуют. А с ними нас не тронут" [Jim, there is nothing we can do. Can't go ashore. This is South. You will be lynched immediately. But with them, they won't touch us].[53] A reference to lynching would not have been new to a Soviet viewer "introduced to the vocabulary of U.S. racism" by the Soviet press even before World War II.[54] But by presenting lynching as a possible outcome for Jim, who has already been established onscreen as a "brother" to the Soviet people, the film underscores the need for an immediate intervention on the part of Huck. So when Jim breaks into tears at the thought that he might never again see his children, Huck responds by hugging Jim and promising he'll help him become free: "Джим, ну не плачь. Заработаем денег, купим билет на пароход, доплывем до Киеро" [Jim, why, don't cry. We'll make money, buy the

---

[53] *Hopelessly Lost*, 48:37–48:50.

[54] Roman, *Opposing Jim Crow*, 60. As Roman notes, American lynch mobs often made Soviet headlines both before and after World War II. Furthermore, Soviet newspapers typically transcribed "lynching" as *linchevat*, instead of substituting an American term with a similar-in-meaning Russian word *samosud* (mob law), to encourage understanding of lynching as "a particularly heinous act of violence peculiar to the advanced capitalist society of the United States" (60).

steamboat tickets, and get to Cairo].[55] Instead of responding with the pangs of remorse over helping a runaway slave, as he previously had, this time Huck commits to helping Jim become free halfway.[56] By stating that "*we*'ll make money" and "*we*'ll get to Cairo," Huck frames Jim's liberation as a communitarian commitment, while the shot of the white and black hands intertwined in an embrace emphasizes Soviet commitment to interracial politics.

When the ending is not the end

Significantly different from the novel, the film's ending becomes a place where, ultimately, the Western evils of a racial capitalist system and the Soviet values of interracial class solidarity collide. With Huck's moral conflict resolved earlier in the film (once he commits to help Jim get to Cairo), the ending does not feature the Phelps's farm segment with Tom Sawyer, or Huck's letter to Miss Watson, or the famous "all right, then, I'll *go* to hell" line.[57] Instead, the ending takes on the shape of a fast-paced adventure story as Huck, who was restocking provisions in town, returns to the raft only to find the Duke drunk, the King and Jim missing, and less than an hour to locate Jim before the steamboat departs for Cairo.

When Huck finally locates Jim, whom the King had sold to a farmer at the edge of town, the entire town is distracted by Sherburn's murder of the drunk Boggs, which allows Huck to sneak into the barn and free Jim, undetected. From this scene of Jim's escape—it is hard to call it a liberation, since Jim still has shackles on his ankles and there is no letter from Miss Watson to set him free in the eyes of the law— the film cuts to the violent mob chasing the tarred-and-feathered King and Duke out of town. In a disturbingly long take, the drunk townsmen are shown laughing and jumping around the tarred conmen, as the sunset colors the entire scene in the hues of black and orange and the non-diegetic sound of war drums blends with the peaceful piano music to underscore the violence of this burlesque.[58] As the camera gives a panoramic shot of the King and Duke rolling down the cliff with the townsmen throwing stones at them, Jim and Huck, who missed the steamboat to Cairo, are seen floating by the shore on their raft. The camera gives a close-up of Jim's face, his eyes

---

[55] *Hopelessly Lost*, 49:18-49:28.

[56] Twain, *Huckleberry Finn*, 215. For comparison, since *Huckleberry Finn* centers around Huck's inner conflict and slow moral growth, Twain's Huck only notes that "[Jim] cared just as much for his people as white folks does for their'n," even though "it don't seem natural."

[57] Twain, *Huckleberry Finn*, 297, emphasis in original.

[58] *Hopelessly Lost*, 1:28:01-1:28:18.

intently watching those who sold him into slavery being beaten. Suddenly, Jim jumps out of his hiding spot on the raft and starts rowing; Huck follows his example. It is unclear in which direction they are moving until the wider shot shows them reaching the shore and helping the King and Duke climb onto the raft. The film ends with Huck and Jim—who still has shackles around his ankles—standing side by side on the raft smiling at each other as the "royals" kneel by their feet attempting to clean themselves up. Moments before the screen cuts to black, Huck's voiceover proudly pronounces his new life goal: "ничего, расшибусь, но помогу Джиму стать вольным" [Well, I'll lay myself out, but I'll help Jim become a free man].[59] The end.

Being the first adaption of *The Adventures of Huckleberry Finn* in which Jim does not end up free, the conclusion of *Hopelessly Lost* requires a thorough examination. When read in the context of the Cold War, the three major points of departure from the novel—first, the exclusion of Tom Sawyer; second, Jim's decision to save "the royals;" and, third, Jim's precarious position in the end— acquire new layers of meaning.

Of course, *Hopelessly Lost* is not the first film adaptation of *The Adventures of Huckleberry Finn* to discard Tom Sawyer. In the 1939 and 1960 American productions, Tom is also noticeably absent. But, if in American versions these alterations signal Americans' discomfort with the burlesque ending of Twain's novel in the context of the approaching war and rising Civil Rights Movement, respectively, Daneliya's decision to exclude Tom from his film sends a different message.[60] By omitting Tom, who sees Jim's rescue as just another game, this ending underscores the grave realities of the American racial order. After all, Tom would not send the right message to the Soviet viewer, since his mischiefs spring from his active imagination nursed by the romantic tradition, rather than a desire to break out of the capitalist system. In contrast, Huck, a more down-to-earth character, who resists "being civilized" by American society, fits well in the Soviet tradition of "ordinary heroes" and "orphan fiction" that "served the highly politicized message of class struggle."[61] Consequently, by excluding Tom from the film's resolution, *Hopelessly Lost* shifts the dynamics of Twain's burlesque ending; with no Tom and his extravagant rescue plan in sight,

---

[59] *Hopelessly Lost*, 1:32:13-1:32:17.

[60] See Frank, *Adventures of Huckleberry Finn on Film*; Newell, "'You don't know about me without you have read a book.'"

[61] Marina Balina, "'It's Grand to be An Orphan!': Crafting Happy Citizens in Soviet Children's Literature of the 1920s," in *Petrified Utopia: Happiness Soviet Style*, eds. E. A. Dobrenko and Marina Balina (New York: Anthem Press, 2009), 105.

Huck emerges as a beacon of morality uncorrupted by the violent culture around him, a true Soviet subversive.

With Huck's character solidified as a metaphor for Soviet racial open-mindedness, the final blow against American racial stereotypes is delivered by Jim. Although it is somewhat idealistic of Daneliya to suggest a runaway slave would want to rescue those who sold him back into slavery, this altercation grants Jim an unprecedented degree of agency, something that, according to critics, the American version of Jim lacks both on page and on screen.[62] Indeed, if in the novel, Jim obediently endures the cruel play of the two white boys, in *Hopelessly Lost*, it is Jim who puts an end to the townsmen's torture of the King and Duke by choosing to save them. In Soviet culture, which prized itself on its value of comradeship, Jim's decision to extend his hand to his oppressors would indicate his moral superiority, and, with it, the superiority of the oppressed races. Indeed, since the King and Duke have previously been established on screen as metaphors for everything that is wrong with contemporary America, their pitiful state at the end of the film—tarred-and-feathered, kneeling by Huck and Jim's feet—indicates the deficiencies of the American way of life. In contrast, Huck and Jim are shown to stand by each other as equals, echoing Aseev's interpretation of the two as "brothers forever" representing the Soviets' anti-racist image.

Yet, the shackles on Jim's feet remind the viewer that the raft is still in Southern territory; although he has escaped the captivity of the barn, Jim is not free in the eyes of the law. When read in the context of the Cold War, such an ending implies that the fight for a socialist international (and interracial) utopia is not over: the African-American brother is still in shackles and must be saved by a Soviet comrade. By not offering the expected happy resolution, *Hopelessly Lost* calls on the Soviet viewer to extend Huck's fight for one slave's freedom into a fight for a better future for workers of all races.

Thus, *Hopelessly Lost* restages the racial conflict of *The Adventures of Huckleberry Finn* as an imperialist conflict between capitalist and communist blocs, appropriating a nineteenth-century American text to Cold War tensions. By reimagining Huck and Jim as a metaphor of socialist interracial alliance, the film extends the Soviet critique against capitalist exploitation of non-whites from the political to the cultural arena. At the same time, this rendition of Twain's classic works to distract Soviets from their own shortcomings regarding

---

[62] For the overview of scholarly debate around the ending of *The Adventures of Huckleberry Finn*, see Jonathan Arac, "All Right, Then, I'll *Go* to Hell: Historical Contexts for Chapter 31," in *Huckleberry Finn as Idol and Target* (Madison: University of Wisconsin Press, 1997), 37-62.

the pursuit of freedom and equality for all; as modern scholarship reminds us, "arbitrary imprisonment; the denial of human rights through the use of inhumane prison conditions and even torture; and the state's use of spies and terror to intimidate potential dissidents, including occasional 'disappearances,' along with antisemitism were realities of life in the Soviet Union that rarely made the papers."[63] Yet, it is not the purpose of this paper to determine how accurately *Hopelessly Lost* represents the realities of the communist regime or the role of people of color in the Soviet experiment. Instead, by recovering the international network of scholarly, literary, and cinematic clusters around Twain's *Huckleberry Finn*, this paper reminds us how texts can serve various purposes in various national contexts and how they can highlight some political and cultural shortcomings, while simultaneously obscuring others. As Russian and American relations once again turn volatile and as the Black Lives Matter movement continues to draw attention to systematic racism in America, it is important to recall what role race played in previous encounters between Russia and the United States.

Works cited

Antsyferova, Olga. "American Studies in Russia." *European Journal of American Studies* 1, no. 1 (January 2006). https://doi.org/10.4000/ejas.366.

Arac, Jonathan. *Huckleberry Finn as Idol and Target: The Functions of Criticism in Our Time*. Madison: University of Wisconsin Press, 1997.

Baldwin, Kate A. *Beyond the Color Line and the Iron Curtain: Reading Encounters between Black and Red, 1922-1963*. Durham: Duke UP, 2002.

Balina, Marina. "'It's Grand to be An Orphan!': Crafting Happy Citizens in Soviet Children's Literature of the 1920s." In *Petrified Utopia: Happiness Soviet Style*, edited by E. A.

Dobrenko and Marina Balina, 99-114. New York: Anthem Press, 2009.

Blair, Walter. *Mark Twain & Huck Finn*. Berkeley: University of California Press, 1962.

Borstelmann, Thomas. *The Cold War and the Color Line: American Race Relations in the Global Arena*. Cambridge: Harvard UP, 2001.

Canby, Vincent. "New Cannes Festival Star: I. F. Stone." *The New York Times*, May 23, 1974, https://www.nytimes.com/1974/05/23/archives/new-cannes-festival-star-i-f-stone.html.

Carew, Joy Gleason. *Blacks, Reds, and Russians: Sojourners in Search of the Soviet Promise*. New Brunswick: Rutgers UP, 2008.

Daneliya, Georgiy (Данелия, Георгий). *Hopelessly Lost*. Mosfilm Studios, 1973.

———. *Безбилетный Пассажир: Байки Кинорежиссёра [A Passenger Without a Ticket: Memoir]*. Moscow: Eksmo, 2006.

---

[63] Borstelmann, *The Cold War and the Color Line*, 4.

Denisova, Liubov, and Irina Mukhina. *Rural Women in the Soviet Union and Post-Soviet Russia.* London: Routledge, 2010.

Dudziak, Mary L. *Cold War Civil Rights: Race and the Image of American Democracy.* Princeton: Princeton UP, 2011.

Evans, Christine. "The 'Soviet Way of Life' as a Way of Feeling. Emotion and Influence on Soviet Central Television in the Brezhnev Era." *Cahiers Du Monde Russe* 56, no. 2-3 (April 2015): 543-569. https://doi.org/10.4000/monderusse.8201.

Fanon, Frantz. *Black Skin, White Masks.* New York: Grove Press, 2008.

Fedorov, Alexander. *Cinema in the Mirror of the Soviet and Russian Film Criticism.* 2nd ed. Moscow: ICO "Information for All," 2019.

Fishkin, Shelley Fisher. *Lighting out for the Territory: Reflections on Mark Twain and American Culture.* Oxford: Oxford UP, 1998.

Frank, Perry. "Adventures of Huckleberry Finn on Film." In *Huck Finn among the Critics: A Centennial Selection,* edited by Thomas M. Inge, 293-313. Frederick: University Publications of America, 1985.

Friedberg, Maurice. "The U.S. in the U.S.S.R.: American Literature through the Filter of Recent Soviet Publishing and Criticism." *Critical Inquiry* 2, no. 3 (Spring 1976): 519-583. https://doi.org/10.1086/447854.

Fulton, Joe B. *Mark Twain Under Fire: Reception and Reputation, Criticism and Controversy, 1851-2015.* Rochester: Camden House, 2016.

Gogol, J. M. "Nikolai Aseev and Mark Twain." *Mark Twain Journal* 16, no. 4 (Summer 1973): 15-16.

Golovskoy, Valery Semenovich. *Behind the Soviet Screen: The Motion-Picture Industry in the USSR, 1972-1982.* Ann Arbor: Ardis, 1986.

Haupt, Clyde V. *Huckleberry Finn on Film: Film and Television Adaptations of Mark Twain's Novel, 1920-1993.* Jefferson: McFarland, 1994.

Howells, William Dean. *My Mark Twain: Reminiscences and Criticisms.* New York: Harper & Bros, 1910.

Keys, Barbara. "An African-American Worker in Stalin's Soviet Union: Race and the Soviet Experiment in International Perspective." *The Historian* 71, no. 1 (Spring 2009): 31-54. https://www.jstor.org/stable/24454160.

Law, Ian. *Red Racisms: Racism in Communist and Post-Communist Contexts.* New York: Springer, 2016.

Layton, Azza Salama. *International Politics and Civil Rights Policies in the United States, 1941-1960.* Cambridge: Cambridge UP, 2000.

Lemon, Alaina. "The Matter of Race." In *Ideologies of Race: Imperial Russia and the Soviet Union in Global Context,* edited by David Rainbow, 59-76. Montreal: McGill-Queen's UP, 2019.

Matusevich, Maxim. "An Exotic Subversive: Africa, Africans and the Soviet Everyday." *Race & Class* 49, no. 4 (April 2008): 57-81. https://doi.org/10.1177/0306396808089288.

———. "Soviet Anti-Racism and Its Discontents: The Cold War Years." In *Alternative Globalizations: Eastern Europe and the Postcolonial World,* edited by James Mark, Artemy M. Kalinovsky, and Steffi Marung, 229-250. Bloomington: Indiana UP, 2020.

Michaels, Paula A. "Navigating Treacherous Waters: Soviet Satire, National Identity, and Georgii Daneliia's Films of the 1970s." *Historical Journal of Film, Radio, and Television* 29, no. 3 (2009): 343-364. https://doi.org/10.1080/0143 9680903145587.

Newell, Kate. "'You don't know about me without you have read a book:' Authenticity in Adaptations of 'Adventures of Huckleberry Finn.'" *Literature/ Film Quarterly* 41, no. 4 (October 2013): 303-316.

Parry, Albert. "Mark Twain in Russia." *Books Abroad* 15, no. 2 (Spring 1941): 168-175. https://doi.org/10.2307/40100322.

Pease, Donald E. *The New American Exceptionalism*. Minneapolis: University of Minnesota Press, 2009.

Proffer, Carl R. *Soviet Criticism of American Literature in the Sixties; an Anthology*. Ann Arbor: Ardis, 1972.

Roman, Meredith L. *Opposing Jim Crow African Americans and the Soviet Indictment of U.S. Racism, 1928-1937*. Lincoln: University of Nebraska Press, 2012.

Schmitz, Neil. "Mark Twain in the Twenty-First Century." *American Literary History* 16, no. 1 (March 2004): 117-126. https://doi.org/10.1093/ALH/AJH007.

Shabad, Theodore. "'Huck Finn' Put on Film in Soviet." *The New York Times*, November 29, 1972. https://www.nytimes.com/1972/11/29/archives/huck-finn-put-on-film-in-soviet.html.

Shaw, Tony, and Denise Jeanne Youngblood. *Cinematic Cold War: The American and Soviet Struggle for Hearts and Minds*. Lawrence: UP of Kansas, 2014.

Smith, Henry Nash. *Introduction to Adventures of Huckleberry Finn*. Boston: Houghton Mifflin, 1958.

Startsev, Abel (Старцев, Абель). *Марк Твен и Америка [Mark Twain and America]*. Moscow: Pravda, 1980.

Stetsenko, Ekaterina A. "Mark Twain in Russian Periodicals. Part 1." *Studia Litterarum* 2, no. 2 (June 2017): 120–143. https://doi.org/10.22455/2500-4247-2017-2-2-120-143.

Trilling, Lionel. *The Liberal Imagination; Essays on Literature and Society*. Garden City: Doubleday, 1953.

Twain, Mark. *The Adventures of Huckleberry Finn*. New York: Harper & Bros., 1912.

Weitz, Eric D. "Racial Politics without the Concept of Race: Reevaluating Soviet Ethnic and National Purges." *Slavic Review* 61, no. 1 (Spring 2002): 1-29. https://doi.org/10.2307/2696978.

Westheider, James E. *Fighting on Two Fronts: African Americans and the Vietnam War*. New York: New York UP, 1997.

Whittaker, Tom, and Sarah Wright. *Locating the Voice in Film: Critical Approaches and Global Practices*. Oxford: Oxford UP, 2016.

Wood, Michael. "The Languages of Cinema." In *Nation, Language, and the Ethics of Translation*, dited by Sandra Bermann and Michael Wood, 79-88. Princeton: Princeton UP, 2005.

Woods, Jeff R. *Black Struggle, Red Scare: Segregation and Anti-Communism in the South, 1948--1968*. Baton Rouge: Louisianna State UP, 2003.

Žižek, Slavoj. "I Hear You With My Eyes." In *Gaze and Voice as Love Objects*. Edited by Renata Salecl and Slavoj Žižek, 90-126. Durham: Duke UP, 1996.

Chapter 5

A world in the margins: *Oscar Wao,* its paratexts, and how we read world literature

Cathryn Piwinski

Rutgers University

Abstract

This essay examines the political and aesthetic characteristics of contemporary "world literature" through the case study of paratexts in Junot Díaz's *The Brief Wondrous Life of Oscar Wao.* Specifically, this paper challenges the definition of "world literature" offered in *n+1 Magazine's* article "World Lite," in which the authors condemn what they claim is an apolitical genre mobilized by publishers to perform multiculturalism. The authors of the article conclude that "world literature" must be replaced by a more politically-combative "internationalist literature." In imagining this dichotomy between "world" and "internationalist," however, the authors dismiss the ambiguous relationships novels have with the publishing industry from which they came and the socio-political nuance of their authors, characters, and readers. The paratexts (marketing blurbs, author biographies, and footnotes) of Díaz's *Oscar Wao* become an important site of this ambiguity. Its paratexts hold traces of a publisher intent on marketing a white-washed Díaz and a vacuous Americanist multiculturalism to gain both commercial success and literary prestige. Yet, the novel simultaneously offers alternative paratexts—footnotes written by a character—that internally resist the American nationalism flanking the narrative. In engaging the formal and political differences between these two sets of paratexts, this paper ultimately argues that Oscar Wao deconstructs the dichotomy between the palatable "world" and the combative "internationalist" literature. This essay concludes with the assertion that, more generally, novels of world literature are already multivalent and productive spaces of socio-political imaginaries, resistance, and contradictions that transcend limits imposed by their local or national publishers.

Keywords: World Literature; Díaz, Junot; Internationalist Literature; Multiculturalism; Paratext

***

In the attempt to define the science fiction genre, Junot Díaz's *The Brief Wondrous Life of Oscar Wao* incidentally offers a definition of world literature. In explaining why his subject, Oscar, is so enamored with science fiction, the narrator Yunior proposes that "living in the DR for the first couple of years of his life and then abruptly wrenchingly relocating to New Jersey" meant that only "the most extreme scenarios could have satisfied."[1] Yunior claims that the genre offers Oscar a sort of identification: "You really want to know what being an X-Man feels like? Just be a smart bookish boy of color in a contemporary U.S. ghetto."[2] Science fiction provides Oscar with stories that incorporate both extreme (here, otherworldly) difference and intimate familiarity. Above all else, science fiction as Yunior defines it is a genre structured by its readers—that is, how readers *connect* their own, perhaps unstable position in the world with the defamiliarizations that occur within science fiction. This relation is a mode of reading that focuses on becoming familiar with new places, new people, new ideas, and new phenomena within both narrative and context. In Oscar's case, this means identifying his own isolation with the estrangement of "an X-Man." In reading science fiction, he reads himself into the text; he uses the genre's themes of coping with difference to make sense of, and even escape, the world in which he finds himself.

Yunior's formulation of science fiction introduces a potential typing of *Oscar Wao* itself as, counterintuitively, less a work of science fiction, but more a work of world literature. The two genres share superficial interests: in explorations or exploitations of places alternate to the Anglophone world, in encounters with an "other" either earnestly engaged with or offensively displayed, and in methods of rethinking how we, the readers, live in these spaces. In world literature specifically, these suspect themes of encounter, exploitation, and exhibitionism at times cross beyond the borders of the narrative and into the presentation, circulation, and reception of the text. As we will come to see, "world literature" is hardly a straightforward term, though critics have understood it varyingly as a grouping of texts read outside of their place of origin, books written in vernacular languages or in languages easily translatable, or all works excluded from a Western canon.[3] Most relevant to this essay, however,

---

[1] Junot Díaz, *The Brief Wondrous Life of Oscar Wao* (New York: Riverhead Books, 2007), 21-22.

[2] Díaz, *Oscar Wao*, 22.

[3] See David Damrosch, *What Is World Literature?* (Princeton: Princeton UP, 2003);

is an understanding of world literature as a genre used by the Anglophone or American publishing industry. Within this context, it is a genre that, perhaps meaningfully at first, foregrounds diversity and difference—for instance, between Oscar's bookishness and Yunior's coolness, the Dominican Republic and the United States, English and Spanish—to promote a commercialized worldliness that sells books. This hyperfocus on marketability and profit deliberately targets a widespread audience of readers and smooths away any political, social, or cultural specificity within the narrative that may prove too controversial for a bestseller list. In other words, while the science fiction novel often targets the science fiction reader, the commercial and palatable world literary novel appeals to any and every reader. Novels of world literature, packaged by and for a mainstream publishing world, come to embody that above-mentioned exhibitionism: different, intriguing, exotic enough, and ultimately made for consumption.

However bleak the state of the world literary novels seems, though, this essay aims to propose a new definition of the genre that recognizes resistance from within the publishing industry, especially on the part of that so-called "every" reader. This reframing incorporates major capitalist players in literary production at the same time as it finds hope in possible readers that, like Oscar, relate to and act on the book's more conflicting internal narratives. World literature, I argue, is a genre belonging to its readers because their role within the genre is so multivalent. At once a targeted, apolitical mass of consumers and a singular, critical, and resistant reader, the audiences of world literature dictate both the book's lifespan in the marketplace and its significance within a larger context of cultural knowledge production and exchange. When we more critically focus on how it directly engages with its myriad readers, world literature becomes a self-aware genre that understands and responds to its own role within the marketplace. In crossing national borders and language barriers, in mixing personal and public identities, and in addressing a diverse and complex audience, world literature demands from its readers thoughtful, meaningful, and active engagement with its contradictory multiplicities.

This essay's resistance to a single understanding of world literature as simply commercial is, in part, a response to ongoing critical skepticism of the literary utility of the genre. This skepticism follows a flurry of world literary scholarship and contests a burgeoning tendency to romanticize the genre as the diversifying

---

Amit Chaudhuri, "Modernity and the Vernacular," in *The Picador Book of Modern Indian Literature* (London: Picador, 2001); Rebecca Walkowitz, "Comparison Literature," *New Literary History* 40, no. 3 (Summer 2009): 567-582, https://www.jstor.org/stable/27760276; and Edward Said, "Humanism's Sphere," *Humanism and Democratic Criticism* (New York: Columbia UP, 2004), 1-30.

antidote to Anglocentric literature. In her book *Against World Literature*, Emily Apter writes: "I do harbor some serious reservations in World Literature."[4] Likewise, the editors of *n+1 Magazine* claim that "it's hard not to be suspicious of anything as wholesome as World Literature."[5] These doubts are likely warranted, as these authors point to the familiar story that "world literature" is a genre produced, circulated, and consecrated by global capitalist industries such as the international publishing house and modern university. In this context, world literary texts are novels used to market an apolitical and palatable multiculturalism and to perform diversity to gain prestige and sell books.[6] This understanding examines not just what novels say about the world, but how they exist as part of a network within the world, relating to both reader and publisher, prevailing aesthetics, and market exploitations. When Apter and the *n+1* editors refer to "world literature," they are referring to a group of novels marketed as "worldly"—books that usually narrate some sort of multicultural difference, but are nonetheless Anglicized or Americanized in their marketing. These are texts deemed different or provocative *enough* to spark a voyeuristic interest by a Western audience, but are ultimately diluted, evacuated of any socio-political and cultural nuance.

While it is not surprising that Apter and the *n+1* editors would be skeptical of such a genre, conclusions drawn about the motivations of the industry around a particular novel should not reduce or dismiss the internal complexity within it. This essay maintains that, at the same time as industries of global capital attempt to manipulate how a text circulates and sells, the works themselves can anticipate and respond to their own complicity in the market. In building a responsible relationship with and calling for action from their readers, these texts can trouble the systems of which they are a part. This relationship is foregrounded in the paratexts, which are spaces of interaction that reveal how an individual text negotiates its relationship with its publisher and reader; examining them enables us to understand how a text responds to both. They

---

[4] Emily Apter, *Against World Literature: On the Politics of Untranslatability* (New York: Verso, 2013), 2.

[5] Mark Krotov and Dayna Tortorici, "World Lite: What is Global Literature?," *n+1 Magazine* 17 (Fall 2013), accessed April 1, 2020, https://nplusonemag.com/issue-17/the-intellectual-situation/world-lite/.

[6] Apter, *Against World Literature*, 2. In referring to "multiculturalism," this essay adopts the definition offered by Waïl S. Hassan, who critiques how the industrialized world literary genre (namely, the manufacturing of unwieldy world literature anthologies) relies upon a *performative* multiculturalism "that superficially [celebrates] difference and diversity while commodifying cultural production" (40). See Waïl S. Hassan, "World Literature in the Age of Globalization: Reflections on an Anthology," *College English* 63, no. 1 (September 2000): 38-47, https://doi.org/10.2307/379030.

also remind readers that *any* work of literature, no matter how critical of its surroundings, is inevitably intertwined with the market. Specifically, this essay will use Junot Díaz's *The Brief Wondrous Life of Oscar Wao* as its case study, as it is both a work of Post45 literature and a novel explicitly cited by the *n+1* editors as a work of agreeable world literature. In its negotiation with its own world "literariness," *Oscar Wao* simultaneously reveals a vexed relationship with the "Americanness" that has come to characterize Post45 novels: its paratexts constrain it to American origins and perspectives at the same time they counterintuitively push the book towards an international market and audience.

This paradox reveals itself when the novel's marketing blurbs show traces of a palatable publishing industry intent on selling a vague, but distinctly American, multiculturalism to gain both commercial success and literary prestige abroad. Yet the novel simultaneously offers alternative paratexts—footnotes written not by a publisher, but by a character—that mount significant resistance to its marketing by presenting alternative ways to understand how both novel and reader exist in the modern, and notably *global*, world. Ultimately, *Oscar Wao* calls for and explicitly models responsible readers, both aware of the market's tendency to exploit, smooth away, or parrot difference, and self-critical of their role in this system. Its competing paratexts show us that the novel of world literature is multivalent, incorporating traces left not only by an Anglocentric commercialized publisher, but also a biased and fallible author and a lazy or activist reader. These paratexts indicate that a world literary novel is one in constant negotiation with its place in a decentered world by responding to its circulation, enabling or opposing its marketing, and calling for a certain methodology of reading: closely, responsibly, exhaustively, and skeptically.

World literature and its paratexts

Paratexts, as defined by Gérard Genette, act as a "threshold" to the book.[7] They "surround and extend [the text], precisely in order to present it... to ensure a text's presence in the world, its 'reception' and *consumption*."[8] Paratexts are marks of book production; they are a means of packaging the text not only to preview the internal narrative, but to promote circulation amongst a public, construct a readership, sell copies, and garner prestige. In this way, paratexts include titles, author names, press blurbs, prize emblems, and price tags, all of

---

[7] Gérard Genette, *Paratexts: Thresholds of Interpretation*, trans. Jane E. Lewin (Cambridge: Cambridge UP, 1997), 1.

[8] Genette, *Paratexts*, 1, emphasis added.

which contribute to a book's value in the market. For instance, while a price tag literally assigns monetary value to a text, the font and size of the author's name may indicate their own celebrity or legitimacy among a readership. A prize emblem claims a certain cultural relevancy or aesthetic mastery within the text, while complimentary press blurbs indicate why the reader should also appreciate the work. Paratexts, then, are powerful sites of marketing. To use Genette's language, the paratext "constitutes a zone... not only of transitions but also of *transaction*: a privileged place of a pragmatics and a strategy, of an influence on the public, an influence that... is at the service of a better reception for the text."[9] The word "transaction" foregrounds the economic or commercial use of paratexts, as well as the various relationships they represent: between reader and text, reader and author, text and publisher, and so on. In short, they embody an often-overlooked node connecting a work of literature to the many actors that influence its composition, material production, and participation in the marketplace. Paratexts, though, reveal more than just a neutral system of relations; they also exist as spaces of debate between them. In the case of world literature, they stage and enable moments of misunderstanding, disagreement, and struggle between a commercial publisher, author, and reader. In other words, paratexts can offer significant spaces for internal negotiations with or in defiance of a text's own generic qualities.

Paratexts, therefore, offer visible evidence to indicate how a work of literature exists within and interacts with the world. Examination of this interaction dovetails with the ongoing debate in literary studies of what "world literature" is, what it does and says and how it does and says it, how it circulates, and by whom and for whom it is written.[10] Franco Moretti's and Pascale Casanova's understanding of world literature, as part of a larger conglomeration of political, economic, and linguistic "worlds," provides an understanding of the genre most relevant to this essay. For them, world literature is a grouping of texts largely in service of facilitating and validating the expansion of elite global

---

[9] Genette, *Paratexts*, 2.

[10] First theorized by Johann Wolfgang von Goethe in the nineteenth century, *Weltliteratur*, or World Literature, was a body of works that crossed national boundaries to construct a more "universal" (but still European) literature that promoted understanding and tolerance between nations (ntd. in Strich 350). Since this coinage, world literature has come to have multiple, and often contradictory meanings, ranging from a discrete collection of texts to a global system of relations, to works written for or in resistance to translation. See Fritz Strich, *Goethe and World Literature*, trans. by C. A. M. Sym (London: Routledge & Kegan Paul Ltd., 1949); Damrosch, *What is World Literature?*; Eric Hayot, "Worlds, Literatures, Systems," in *On Literary Worlds* (Oxford: Oxford UP, 2012), 30-42; Walkowitz, "Comparison Literature;" and Chaudhuri, "Modernity and the Vernacular."

capitalism.[11] Although world literature "as an elite commodity" is by no means a new definition, Sarah Brouillette notes that the 2013 publications of Apter's *Against World Literature* and *n+1*'s "World Lite" invigorated this critique leveled at the genre.[12] Essentially, Brouillette writes, these pieces proposed that "world literature" has "for decades applied to a canon of classics curated by acquisitive publishers located in the West."[13] These critics claim that world literature is a tool by which industries of global capitalism (the publishing industry and the modern university) perform multicultural values to maximize their economic reach. Here, we see the necessary intermingling of the world literary industry and the world literary genre; in incorporating an understanding of literature as always interacting with other "worlds" (of politics, of economics, etc.) we find the genre is *also* constituted by how it is made and how it is read. The genre of world literature, then, is determined both by what is within its narratives and the methods by which the publishing industry negotiates, presents, and disseminates them.

The realization that world literature is a genre always intertwined with the exploitative markets of global capitalism is an inevitably demoralizing one. The *n+1* editors point out that world literature is a deceptive genre, in which any political complexity or social radicalism is swapped out for elitism, gutted of any controversy by the publisher and university, and in actuality is written for a small audience.[14] It is, they write, a genre engineered and upheld by industries of Western global capital, with:

> ... its signature writers: Rushdie and Coetzee at the lead, and Kiran Desai, Mohsin Hamid, and Chimamanda Ngozi Adichie among the younger charges. It has its own economy, consisting of international publishing networks, scouts, and book fairs. It has its prizes: the Nobel, of course, but more powerful and snazzier is the Man Booker, and Man Booker International. Its political arm is PEN. And it has a social calendar full of literary festivals, which bring global elites into contact with the glittering stars of World Lit...... What happens at these festivals? No debate; no yelling; some drinking; lots of signing of books. They are like peace conferences.[15]

---

[11] Hayot, "Worlds, Literatures, Systems," 31.

[12] Sarah Brouillette, "On Some Recent Worrying over World Literature's Commodity Status," *Maple Tree Literary Supplement*, no. 18 (December 2014), accessed August 15, 2020, http://www.mtls.ca/issue18/impressions/.

[13] Brouillette, "On Some Recent Worrying over World Literature's Commodity Status."

[14] Krotov and Tortorici, "World Lite."

[15] Krotov and Tortorici, "World Lite."

Rather than risk any legitimate critique of its complicity in global capitalism, the editors claim, publishers instead manufacture a "glittering" and performative world literature to, under the guise of multiculturalism, act as "an empty vessel for the occasional self-ratification of the global elite."[16] The performative intention of the industry is therefore reproduced within the narratives of world literature. In other words, world literature as a genre becomes less a means by which the industry and its readers examine their own relationship to the world, and more the tool by which global industry validates and disguises its own elitism.

Although, as one commenter writes in response to "World Lite," the article ushered in a "brouhaha" of critiques for their hopelessness of tone, their reduction of literary history, and their vague terminology, their general claim that world literature is an easily consumable genre made for global market seems largely accepted.[17] What encourages a primary thread of disagreement amongst responses, however, is the editors' final suggestion that we (as critics, scholars, consumers, and readers) forsake world literature altogether and focus on an entirely new genre called "internationalist literature." Internationalist literature, the editors claim, is a genre penned by the "revolutionary left," which manifests in "a given vernacular but [is] always aimed at a borderless audience of radicals."[18] Dichotomous to world literature, which they insist is a corporate "product," internationalist literature is a "project," a genre decoupled from the industry and characterized by an ongoing process of aesthetic and political

---

[16] Krotov and Tortorici, "World Lite." This is an indictment made often by other critics beyond what we have already seen from Apter. See Aamir R. Mufti, "Orientalism and the Institution of World Literatures," *Critical Inquiry* 36 (2010): 458-493, https://doi.org.10.1086/653408; and Tabish Khair, "Death of the Reader," *OPEN Magazine*, October 2011, https://openthemagazine.com/essays/arts-letters/death-of-the-reader/.

[17] See the following blog posts and commentaries: Amardeep Singh, "On N+1's 'World Lite,'" *Electrostani* (blog), August 27, 2013, http://www.electrostani.com/2013/08/on-n1s-world-lite.html; Jennifer Solheim, "n+1's World Lite: A Hopeful Response," *Jennifer Solheim* (blog), August 17, 2013, https://jennifersolheim.com/2013/08/17/n1s-world-lite-a-hopeful-response/; Gloria Fisk, "Against World Literature: The Debate in Retrospective," *The American Reader*, accessed August 15, 2020, https://theamericanreader.com/against-world-literature-the-debate-in-retrospect/; and Poorva Rajaram and Michael Griffith, "Why World Literature Looks Different in Brooklyn," *3 Quarks Daily* (blog), https://3quarksdaily.com/3quarksdaily/2013/08/why-world-literature-looks-different-from-brooklyn.html. See also, *n+1 Magazine*'s response to these criticisms: Krotov and Tortorici, "'The Rest is Indeed Horseshit,' Pt. 6: On World Lit #BEEF," *n+1 Magazine* (2013), accessed August 15, 2020, https://www.nplusonemag.com/online-only/horseshit/the-rest-is-indeed-horseshit-pt-6/.

[18] Krotov and Tortorici, "World Lite."

reinvention, an inherent opposition to "prevailing tastes, ways of writing, and politics," and a devotion to what they call "truth."[19] Yet, as Brouillette argues, imagining a genre independent of, or at least consistently revolting against, the market's influence seems a fraught exercise. In calling for an insurrectionary genre resistant to the co-option of capitalism, the editors "[fail] to acknowledge that the production of literature is itself fundamentally determined by capitalist social relations."[20] "If critics want to locate and valorize a kind of culture that will not be so readily available to easy market appropriation," Brouillette writes, "they may not be giving the market enough credit."[21] Whatever alternative genre the *n+1* editors offer, its very nature of existing within a capitalist system of literary production will always risk it becoming subsumed once more within the genre of "world literature."

Yet, I suggest that a close reading of these texts demonstrates that this co-option can operate in both directions. If we accept Brouillette's assertion that the market will always find methods to subsume fringe works into its more consumable genres, then it is worth thinking about how these seemingly more combative texts operate within the world literary genre and how they, perhaps, mount resistance from the inside. In conceding that literary production is always or eventually intertwined within the market, I hope to show that certain texts of the world literary genre are self-reflexive; that they are aware of their commodification and work to undo it within their narratives. This exercise returns us to paratexts of world literature and a methodology of close reading, which is often overlooked by the genre's theorists.[22] Viewing world literature at a distance, however, risks distraction by patterns that ignore nuance within individual works. In zooming in on the language of world literary texts, we find that sweeping generalizations about the total pacifism of an entire genre may be overstated. Instead, we can find an internal critique that offers a mode of reading the novel not only against its immediate packaging, but also against its

---

[19] Krotov and Tortorici, "World Lite."

[20] Brouillette, "On Some Recent Worrying over World Literature's Commodity Status."

[21] Broulliette, "On Some Recent Worrying over World Literature's Commodity Status."

[22] For example, the editors of "World Lite" tend to name-drop authors and outline their historical trajectories, rather than engage in any long-form reading of their works. This method of analysis within world literature is perhaps due to Franco Moretti's call for "distant reading," a practice inaugurated in response to his claim that "reading 'more' seems hardly to be the solution" for coming to understand what world literature is (55). Instead, he offers "distant reading," in which the critique seldom engages directly with a text, but instead identifies patterns that exist beyond and across multiple texts (57). See Franco Moretti, "Conjectures on World Literature," *New Left Review* 1 (January/February 2000): 54-68.

context within the world at large. This, in turn, ennobles a more nuanced approach to the industry that enables the genre and how a reader operates within it.

Focusing specifically on the paratexts of a novel and how the novel's internal narrative responds to and reworks those framing devices ensures that a close reading of the language of the novel simultaneously accounts for its context. While we can find traces of this paratextual tension across works of world literature, this essay takes up one case study, Díaz's *Oscar Wao*, for several reasons.[23] First, the novel incorporates two different sets of paratexts: its more traditional, marketing paratexts flanking the novel and its diegetic paratexts (footnotes written by a character), which together expose a tension helpful to understanding how narrative and context chafe against one another. Second, the marketing paratexts show a performative multiculturalism as they attempt to white-wash Díaz and Americanize his novel. Third and finally, Díaz, formerly one of the "glittering stars" of the world literary publishing sphere for his "provocative," but fictional novels, is now more controversial and absent from the public, having been accused by multiple women of sexual assault in 2018. These reasons work together to reveal the paradoxes inherent to the work of the world literature: contradictory ideas held within a single narrative, the faux-diversity of publishing industries as they publish genuinely diverse works, celebrated and maligned authors who hold simultaneously too much power (to exploit others) and too little (to resist global capital). These contradictions (too "thorny" to be smoothed entirely away by the industry's mechanisms manipulating the genre) are dumped in the lap of the reader, a figure who, ultimately, comes to embody and enact what the world literary genre actually

---

[23] For example, a reader's guide for Chinua Achebe's *Things Fall Apart* prompts a reductive, and notably Anglicanized, understanding of the text: characterizing the nine egwugwu as the "Supreme Court" and asking the reader to evaluate the "advantages and disadvantages" of the "Ibo religious structure" when compared to their own. At the same time, the actual content of the novel, which offers a multivocality that resists a monolithic portrait of "African" culture, religion, or tradition, refuses the essentialization proposed in the guide. Similarly, the ongoing (paratextual) debates around the English translation of Han Kang's *The Vegetarian* are complicated beyond simple syntactic accuracy when the text asks us to consider the untranslatability of both tone-shifts between characters and South Korean food culture contextualizing the novel. See Claire Armistead, "Lost in (mis)translation? English takes on Korean novel has critics up in arms," *The Guardian*, January 15, 2018, https://www.theguardian.com/books/booksblog/2018/jan/15/lost-in-mistranslation-english-take-on-korean-novel-has-critics-up-in-arms; and Jiayang Fan, "Han Kang and the Complexity of Translation," *The New Yorker*, January 8, 2018, https://www.newyorker.com/magazine/2018/01/15/han-kang-and-the-conplexity-of-translation.

is. In other words, world literature refuses a simplification of categories. Allowed to be neither fully American nor fully international in the scope of its paratexts, *Oscar Wao* instead negotiates between both "worlds" that characterize the world literary genre. Because this genre both embodies institutions of power and critiques them, it requires a method of reading closely that prompts a perpetual critique of these Anglocentric institutions, as well as a self-reflexivity of how one reads, how one is complicit or resistant, and how one exists, just like the novel, in the world.

Palatability in the paratexts of *Oscar Wao*

In many ways, Díaz once epitomized what "World Lite" sees as world literature: winner of a Pulitzer and holding a faculty position at MIT (for the *n+1* editors, the university is the primary authority ratifying the world literary genre), this "glittering star" was just Dominican *enough* to peddle the industry's so-called multiculturalism, but just American enough to market over it. The editors take aim at Díaz several times in the essay, claiming that his texts concentrate on "historical trauma" rather than critique contemporary global capital.[24] *Oscar Wao*, they claim, "turns abruptly from the lives of contemporary Dominican Americans to their painful background in the Trujillo dictatorship," a period in history that most, if not all, liberal readers would agreeably find heinous.[25] This focus on non-controversial history, however, "[displaces] the contemporary world, locating politics always *elsewhere*, in some distant geography and irrecoverable past."[26] In essence, *Oscar Wao* does not transgress *enough* to disqualify its participation in global literary production. Here, we might disagree with the editors, responding that categorizing *Oscar Wao* as inoffensive is counterintuitive: the text is populated with explicit language, slurs, misogyny, and racism that might disqualify the text from the world literary genre for being too socially or politically contentious. But *Oscar Wao*'s obscenities are one-dimensional; there is little complexity to what is moral and what is wrong.[27]

---

[24] Krotov and Tortorici, "World Lite."

[25] Krotov and Tortorici, "World Lite."

[26] Krotov and Tortorici, "World Lite."

[27] Also published in *n+1*, Bruce Robbins's "Bad Atrocity Writing" claims a certain imprecision present in disaster writing, a genre of writing that is intentionally offensive and graphic and thus encourages readers to either skim these moments (thereby missing the inherent unreliability of the situation) or to resist these moments (making "dead-baby jokes" that avoid any "strong-arming" of their emotions). Like the one-dimensional offensiveness or "safety" of the non-controversial past of *Oscar Wao*, these atrocious descriptions let a reader distance themselves from both the events of the narrative and the method by which it is presented. See Bruce Robbins, "Bad Atrocity Writing," *n+1*

Yunior's persistent womanizing is quickly labeled a character flaw, with him admitting that he was "too much the mess" to maintain a healthy relationship.[28] It can be convincingly argued that the text reproduces sexism and racism to a fault; yet, in terms specific to how the novel is presented to its reader, the bluntness of *Oscar Wao*'s excessive obscenity invites swift denunciation of characters' language and behavior. Just as the novel's focus on the Trujillo dictatorship "[locates] politics always *elsewhere*," so too does the disproportionate obscenity of the novel's language and themes ignore social nuance and invite easy judgment.[29] *Oscar Wao*—from its rehearsal of slurs to its conclusive celebration ("The beauty! The beauty!") of Oscar stalking a woman until she cared, or performed care, for him—does not explore scales of its obscenity or consider its presence in either American or Dominican culture (or the text itself), nor implicate the reader in its reproduction.[30] Instead, it presents an offensiveness designed to be promptly dismissed to a distant "elsewhere."

The claim of a one-dimensional offensiveness, however, is not made to dismiss the problematics of writing obscenity for the sake of obscenity. Rather, it accounts for the work done to smooth out this sharp offense of *Oscar Wao* within the paratext: press blurbs scattered across the first several pages of the novel repackage its vulgarity in ambivalent language like "messy," "unruly," "manic," "flammable," and "giddily glorious and hauntingly horrific." This repackaging reveals the publisher's attempts to control and market the apparent "vibrancy" within the narrative. To this end, the paperback edition of *Oscar Wao* is packed with an absurd amount of marketing paratext. The covers include six press blurbs, which inundate the back cover with text that overpowers the plot summary. Inside, there are *ten more pages* of blurbs, praising not just *Oscar Wao*, but Díaz's other two books: *This Is How You Lose Her* and *Drown*. The front cover bears a loud "*NEW YORK TIMES* BESTSELLER" at the top, capitalized and typeset in a pink color that stands out, and reproduces the "Winner of the Pulitzer Prize" emblem twice (on the cover and the spine). To not consume the novel, then, is to alienate oneself from a significant literary event in history. And it is a clearly persuasive argument, resulting in "weekly sales [that] didn't dip below 5,000 until April 2009" after its paperback release in September 2008 and the overall swift canonization of Díaz

---

Magazine 32 (2018), accessed December 17, 2020, https://nplusonemag.com/issue-32/politics/bad-atrocity-writing/.

28 Díaz, *Oscar Wao*, 324.

29 Krotov and Tortorici, "World Lite."

30 Díaz, *Oscar Wao*, 335.

and his texts in both the commercial literary and academic fields.[31] What these paratexts likewise reveal is *Oscar Wao*'s value to the publishing industry and a significant investment in the book's ability to circulate at an international scale. Yet, at the same time as the awards (the Pulitzer and the Anisfield-Wolf) and press blurbs (from the *New York Times* and *The Boston Globe*) carry weight globally and speak to an international audience, it is notable that nearly all these accolades originate from the United States. Here, we begin to see *Oscar Wao*'s identity solidify as a novel of the contradictory world literary industry: though looking to circulate within the world market, we see once more a firm loyalty to American origins and perspectives.

Díaz himself is also advertised within the paratext of *Oscar Wao*, presented as an author of contemporary America, while also signifying a palatable diversity essential to the world literary industry. His is a simplified advertisement, revealing the publisher's desire to smooth out the complexity of its author and transform him into an apolitical representative of world literature. His name on both the cover and spine of *Oscar Wao* is notably large (and, on the spine, is larger than the book title), indicating that his name holds some recognizable value in literary society. Similarly, the blurbs and backmatter outlining the celebration of his other works show that the paratext is interested in selling the author alongside his novels. In its strangest move, the backmatter incorporates two biographical sections, one more traditional "About the Author," and the other making an explicit argument for Díaz's legitimacy as an artist and his relevance to a global audience:

> Junot Díaz is an American original. He writes as if he's discovered a new language, with a voice so supple and electric and deliriously funny it seems to come from another world. His vision is both panoramic and personal, unflinching and unbearably tender. In his books he maps the hopes, doubts, dreams, and terrible losses of the New America. He embraces the struggling lovers and dreamers, geeks and outsiders at the center of his stories with honesty so intimate it's the highest form of compassion, and captures in them, in all of us, our inextinguishable longings—for home, for hope, for love.[32]

Attributed to no specific author, this paragraph seems articulated by some disembodied, universal, and therefore undeniable voice, not just speaking for

---

[31] Gale Habash, "Just How Much Does a Pulitzer Prize Help a Book's Sales?," *Publishers Weekly*, April 19, 2012, https://www.publishersweekly.com/pw/by-topic/industry-news/awards-and-prizes/article/51573-just-how-much-does-a-pulitzer-prize-help-a-book-s-sales.html.

[32] Díaz, *Oscar Wao*, 343.

the publisher, but for "all of us." At the same time, it conflates this universalism of both author and opinion of the author with both Americanness and an exotified otherworldliness. The paratext oddly claims Díaz as an "American original," further complicating what "American" comes to signify: less a self-contained nation and more a limitless conglomeration of identities akin to the diversity performed in the Anglophone world literary industry. This is biographically incorrect and consequently whitewashes Díaz's Dominican origins in service of a more romanticized and multicultural America. This multicultural America (ostensibly the "New America" to which the text refers) is counterintuitively evacuated of cultural or racial nuance, and the only way Díaz can come to represent it is to become entirely American (and emphatically *not* Dominican-American). This passage's odd conflation between a universalizing but nationalist voice and between a multicultural America and a whitewashed America indicates the novel's tendencies towards the palatability characteristic of world literature. At once feigning universalism in its accounting for a multicultural group of readers and expressing its favoritism towards a reductive, distilled Americanness, this paratextual moment emphasizes *Oscar Wao*'s larger circulation as a world literary product: a novel that operates at an international scale, just as it is framed under a nationalist aesthetic.

At this point, it seems that *Oscar Wao*'s participation in the world literary genre is less due to its own narrative and more symptomatic of its creation within the publishing industry, underlining the idea that world literature is a genre inculcated by global industry. By close reading paratext, we find that much of the argument made towards the novel's universality, value, and agreeability is proposed in the extra-diegetic material. It is worth reiterating that the authors of front and backmatter are seldom made clear (though most likely written by a marketing team) and thereby feign an unbiasedness that sets the expectation and *politics* of the text before the narrative encounter. It is this faux-universal voice that controls and primes the novel of world literature for selected consumption.

This same aim for agreeability means that a world literary publisher may decrease its involvement when a text (or its author) becomes too controversial. In 2018, when Díaz was accused of sexual misconduct, he swiftly disappeared from the public eye. No longer the industry's uncomplicated "glittering star" of world literature, but a complex figure associated with violence, Díaz became no longer palatable enough to represent the global author.[33] This troubles the

---

[33] Since the initial writing of this essay in early 2020, Díaz had all but vanished from the public after the accusations made in May of 2018. His events and book talks were canceled, his social media pages deleted, and his professional website had not been updated since March of 2018 (an announcement for his, at the time, new children's book

world literary genre's tendency to unquestionably celebrate its authors and publishers: Díaz's alleged exploitation of others suggests complicity in the market and the power it affords him, just as it simultaneously reveals the inherent violence of the world literary publisher as an institution that avoids confrontation with an often damaging and always complicated world.[34] When Díaz was accused of reproducing, rather than critiquing, the misogynist behavior displayed by his narrator Yunior, the narrative contained within *Oscar Wao* becomes less charmingly "unruly," and more immediately troublesome. Confronted with a paratext that could not be controlled and smoothed away by language describing Díaz's "honesty" and "compassion," his publishers at Riverhead chose to ignore it and decline comment.[35] This is all to show that a world literary industry, characterized by myths of inclusivity and diversity, shies away from difficulty: just as the books market a one-dimensional view of a multicultural world, so too must their authors remain consumable.

Islandborn). Though he was cleared of misconduct by both the Pulitzer board and MIT, Riverhead Books (his publisher) has made no public comment on the accusations or his relative absence from the literary scene. Since, Díaz has quietly returned to publishing: he wrote, for instance, three book reviews for the *New York Times* in February 2020, February 2021, and October 2021. In July of 2021, he was nominated for a spot in the New Jersey Hall of Fame. The long disappearance from both the Internet and literary circuit, along with his relatively quiet reintroduction into the press, has effectively removed him from the global literary limelight.

[34] In many ways, Díaz has become emblematic of the #MeToo movement in both the university and the publishing industry, sparking debate on how faculty, students, and readers should engage with authors accused of sexual violence. In continuing to write about Díaz, this essay advocates for an open discussion about canonized authors and the violence they have enacted and perpetuated. Readers, I will come to argue, are capable of responsibly working with a text, confronting its, its author's, and its industries' complicity in exploitative practice. There is ongoing and necessary debate over how critics and classrooms should engage with Díaz post-accusations. See Tom Porter, "To Teach or Not to Teach? Nadia Celis on #MeToo and Junot Díaz," *Bowdoin*, October 14, 2019, https://www.bowdoin.edu/news/2019/10/to-teach-or-not-to-teach-nadia-celis-on-metoo-and-junot-d%C3%Adaz.html; Colleen Flaherty, "Junot Díaz, Feminism and Ethnicity," *Inside Higher Ed*, May 29, 2018, https://www.insidehighered.com/news/2018/05/29/rift-among-scholars-over-treatment-junot-d%C3%ADaz-he-faces-harassment-and-misconduct; and Emma Goldberg, "Suitable for the Classroom? #MeToo Spurs a Rethinking," *The New York Times*, October 8, 2019.

[35] Alexandra Alter, Jonah Engel Bromwich, and Damien Cave, "The Writer Zinzi Clemmons Accuses Junot Díaz of Forcibly Kissing Her," *The New York Times*, May 4, 2018, https://www.nytimes.com/2018/05/04/books/junot-diaz-accusations.html?auth=login-email&login=email.

Alternative paratexts, alternative readings

Yet, resigning "world literature" to a grouping of vaguely multicultural texts, made easily consumable by commercial publishing for undiscerning readers, reduces what that "world" encompasses. A more productive understanding of the genre incorporates how the internal mechanisms of the texts can embolden alternative and responsible readings. Even as the paratexts around the novel market both *Oscar Wao* and Díaz as uncomplicated, if a little "messy," figures emblematic of multicultural modern America, there is a second set of paratexts, embedded within the narrative fiction of the work, that resists such a simple taxonomy. Traditionally, footnotes are paratexts that inhabit a space outside of a text's main story or argument. But *Oscar Wao*'s footnotes, already a destabilizing inclusion in a fiction text, play with this formulation when they are attributed in the narrative not to Díaz, but to the narrator Yunior. This creates another collection of paratexts that chafe against the more commercialized paratexts that surround the story and enable a second textual "threshold" more insulated from the whims of the publishing industry.[36] While the backmatter of *Oscar Wao* insists on some vague multicultural Americanness, Yunior's first footnote instead takes aim at a complicit American reader. "For those of you who missed your mandatory two seconds of Dominican history," he writes before plotting out Trujillo's dictatorship, thus calling out the American education system for offering so little information on the Dominican Republic and the American reader disinterested in learning for themselves.[37] In this way, Yunior offers a reading against the grain of the paratexts proper: almost predicting the racist erasure of Díaz's Dominicanness in the backmatter, Yunior in turn emphasizes its relevance to *Oscar Wao*. It follows that the reader must not only account for a multinational experience and perspective, but also confront why this is elided in its institutional context.

Yunior both models a reading against the grain of the palatable world literary paratexts of *Oscar Wao* and stages the opposite: an ignorant, and therefore ineffective, world literary reader. I use "ignorant" here in the same sense as Tabish Khair. In his article "Death of the Reader," he describes a reader of this new, inoffensive (and, he claims, historically inaccurate) world literature. This reader is one "without-History," a "non-reader, as a passive receptor, as a

---

[36] Allison Fagan notes that *Oscar Wao* resists publisher control through a lack of a different paratext: namely, a glossary that would serve to translate the Spanish words used throughout the novel. This absence, per Fagan, refuses "comfort" to monolingual American readers "who clamor for transparency" in their books (63). See Allison Fagan, "Translating in the Margins: Attending to Glossaries in Latina/o Literature," *Journal of Modern Literature* 39, no. 3 (Spring 2016): 57-75, https://doi.org/10.2979/jmodelite.39.3.05.

[37] Díaz, *Oscar Wao*, 2.

simple celebrator of the text, not as someone who interprets, guesses and digs."[38] They fall victim to "a kind of soft 'Western multicultural' ethos" that "usurps... realities and realisations, while enabling the First World reader to experience a fully legible (and, hence, fraudulent) otherness that... privileges the centrality of the European bridge between times and cultures."[39] In the case of *Oscar Wao*, we can read "European" as "American," as the outer paratexts erase the "realities and realisations" of a Dominican or Dominican-American perspective for its interpolated American reader. Yet, as we saw above, the story is not quite so straightforward when the control of the paratexts is passed to Yunior. In the footnotes, he later presents the reader with a sharply critical biography of Abelard, Oscar's grandfather, who lived and died under the Trujillo dictatorship. Though Abelard is not an American reader, he is a wealthy and well-connected one, afforded political and social power at a local level reminiscent of the more international, elitist reader of which Khair speaks. Yet, instead of interrogating his power, Yunior tells us in another footnote that "Abelard had a reputation for being able to keep his head *down* during the worst of the regime's madness—for unseeing as it were."[40] Most importantly, Abelard is an embodiment of that educated, powerful, yet ultimately lazy reader. "While genocide was, in fact, in the making," Yunior continues, "Abelard kept his head, eyes, and nose safely tucked into his books."[41] This desire to engage only with the literary, as opposed to the actual, world results in complete devastation to Abelard's family as the Trujillo regime tortures him, kills his family, and perhaps curses the generations to come. Yunior's paratextual invective against Abelard's disengagement is also critiquing any equally disinterested reader of *Oscar Wao*. This is a reader who, instead of reading the skeptically and critically, accepts the one-dimensional worldview proffered by the novel's paratexts (and contexts). Yunior implicitly reminds his own reader to avoid behaving like Abelard, a reader refusing to deal with the messiness of their own world, and to instead be more confrontational: to read with an awareness of nuance and a readiness to apply what is learned within the text to their own reality. In offering up this resistance to the whitewashing deployed in the extra-diegetic paratexts, *Oscar Wao*'s footnotes condition the reader to actively approach the literally marginal, yet nonetheless supremacist, narratives suspiciously.

---

[38] Khair, "Death of the Reader."

[39] Khair, "Death of the Reader."

[40] Díaz, *Oscar Wao*, 215.

[41] Díaz, *Oscar Wao*, 215.

In so doing, Yunior's footnotes destabilize the presumed authority in the framing paratexts. [42] Leah McCormack writes that in "choosing to insert... history in footnotes, rather than work it into the narrative, Díaz is... discomfiting the reader and thus pushing her... towards a rethinking of the process of narrative—that is, of how stories, and histories, come to be told, by whom and why." [43] In other words, Yunior's footnotes demonstrate how restorative or resistant stories and histories are pushed to the margins. The content of these paratexts challenge both a narrative and historical authority (a nationalist or an Americanist supremacy displayed in *Oscar Wao*'s backmatter) when he reiterates questions of how Dominican history is remembered: "You didn't know we [the Dominican Republic] were occupied twice [by America] in the twentieth century? Don't worry, when you have kids, they won't know the U.S. occupied Iraq either." [44] Yunior is here pointing out to the reader a pattern of omissions of America's imperialist violence; these erasures characterize the nation as complex but ultimately wholesome, as the "New America" celebrated in the backmatter for its "hopes, doubts, dreams" and, noncommittally, "terrible losses." Once more, as Yunior accuses American educational systems and public imaginaries of simplifying history in favor of a nationalist mythos, he simultaneously encourages an equally critical reading of the novel's similarly simplistic and supremacist paratexts. In presenting an alternate account of events "for those of [us] who missed" them, via the voice of an unreliable and fallible narrator and through a reworked formal device, *Oscar Wao* uses its internal paratexts to simulate and suggest a readerly skepticism of its context. [45] Yunior's footnotes begin the work of deconstructing over-arching supremacist narratives and proposing alternate, more holistic methods of storytelling, which he then passes along to the reader. Modeling methods of critique, *Oscar Wao*'s internal paratexts proffer a way of reading not just the novel, but the world in which it exists: with skepticism, nuance, and a critical eye always on global authority.

---

[42] In her foundational article on African American art and its paratexts, Beth A. McCoy advocates for a more critical reading of the margins and how they reproduce and legitimize white supremacy. In engaging texts more analytically, she writes, readers can come to realize "how white power might be transacted through such inconsequential spaces" (158). See Beth A. McCoy, "Race and the (Para)textual Condition," *PMLA: Special Topic: The History of the Book and the Idea of Literature* 121, no. 1 (January 2006), 156-169, https://www.jstor.org/stable/25486294.

[43] Leah McCormack, "Reclaiming Silenced and Erased Histories: The Paratextual Devices of Historic Metafiction," *Making Connections* 14, no. 2 (Fall 2013), 48.

[44] Díaz, *Oscar Wao*, 19.

[45] Díaz, *Oscar Wao*, 2.

Conclusion: margins, recentered

Critical of the institutionally generated and noncontroversial paratexts, as well as modeling the uselessness of an ignorant reader of world literature, Yunior as the narrator of *Oscar Wao* offers a nuanced reading of the world than the *n+1* editors admit. Yunior and his paratexts target a community of authors, readers, and publishers to encourage more confrontational perspectives. As an exemplar of world literature, *Oscar Wao* is a multivalent text: authored by a once-consumable, now controversial figure, marketed by a global publisher interested in garnering prestige and making money, and read by an audience that will choose, per their own position and bias, which paratexts they believe. *Oscar Wao* itself stages this multiplicity in presenting two sets of paratexts that disagree on how to read a book.[46] It contains traces of its own complicity in global capital with paratexts intent on performing diversity, rather than engaging with actual human difference, at the same time as it resists its exploitation when it internally confronts methods of reading and its own readers' ways of living in an unjust world.

In modeling possible readings (some of which are more responsible than others) of its paratexts, *Oscar Wao* offers its own readers a way to critique both the genre's and their own participation in a global literary system. World literature, as a genre always intertwined with the industry that composes and disseminates it, here becomes a collection of texts characterized by their interior and exterior tensions: their multiple loyalties to both internationalism and Americanism, their drive to inform on injustice and to excuse passivity, their desire to both engage and look away from difference. In working simultaneously with and against global capitalist industries, the myth of multiculturalism, and uncomfortable politics, the novel of world literature inhabits multiple spaces, interpolates multiple communities of readers, and reckons with contradictions that exist both inside and outside its narrative world. *Oscar Wao* reminds readers that, even if displaced to the margins of a text, nationalism and white supremacy enable global capital, and vice versa. To

---

[46] *Oscar Wao* is not the only novel of world literature that stages multiplicity in its formal makeup. Han Kang's *The Vegetarian* uses italics to contrast character points-of-view and authority, thus visualizing divergence in vocabulary, tone, and reality. J. M. Coetzee's *Diary of a Bad Year* features three separate narratives, separated by lines, on each page to literally draw barriers between each narrator's thoughts, underlining their conflicting conclusions of a single event. Yaa Gyasi's *Homegoing* alternates essays between two families, tracing generations in Ghana and America to make a point that lives lived under colonization, imperialism, and capitalism take varying forms. All these books, like *Oscar Wao*, experiment with form to question narrative authority and encourage readings that account for a multiplicity of meanings that do not necessarily coincide.

read these texts as texts of world literature means to understand how they exist in a world, how they respond and interact with the world, and how they incorporate and resist the world, which, like its texts, is always composed of spatial, political, economic, and ideological tension. To read these texts as world literature means to also read how we exist, incorporate, and resist that world too.

Works cited

Achebe, Chinua. *Things Fall Apart*. London: Penguin, 1959.

Alter, Alexandra, Jonah Engel Bromwich, and Damien Cave. "The Writer Zinzi Clemmons Accuses Junot Díaz of Forcibly Kissing Her." *The New York Times*, May 4, 2018. https://www.nytimes.com/2018/05/04/books/junot-diaz-accusations.html?auth=login-email&login=email.

Apter, Emily. *Against World Literature: On the Politics of Untranslatability*. New York: Verso, 2013.

Armistead, Claire. "Lost in (mis)translation? English takes on Korean novel has critics up in arms." *The Guardian*, January 15, 2018. https://www.theguardian.com/books/booksblog/2018/jan/15/lost-in-mistranslation-english-take-on-korean-novel-has-critics-up-in-arms.

Brouillette, Sarah. "On Some Recent Worrying over World Literature's Commodity Status." *Maple Tree Literary Supplement*, no. 18 (December 2014). Accessed August 15, 2020. http://www.mtls.ca/issue18/impressions/.

Chaudhuri, Amit. "Modernity and the Vernacular." In *The Picador Book of Modern Indian Literature*, xvii-xxxi. London: Picador, 2001.

Coetzee, J. M. *Diary of a Bad Year*. London: Penguin, 2007.

Damrosch, David. *What Is World Literature?* Princeton: Princeton UP, 2003.

Díaz, Junot. *The Brief Wondrous Life of Oscar Wao*. New York: Riverhead Books, 2007.

Fagan, Allison. "Translating in the Margins: Attending to Glossaries in Latina/o Literature." *Journal of Modern Literature* 39, no. 3 (Spring 2016): 57-75. https://doi.org/10.2979/jmodelite.39.3.05.

Fan, Jiayang. "Han Kang and the Complexity of Translation." *The New Yorker*, January 8, 2018. https://www.newyorker.com/magazine/2018/01/15/han-kang-and-the-complexity-of-translation.

Fisk, Gloria. "Against World Literature: The Debate in Retrospect." *The American Reader*. Accessed August 15, 2020. http://theamericanreader.com/against-world-literature-the-debate-in-retrospect/.

Flaherty, Colleen. "Junot Díaz, Feminism and Ethnicity." *Inside Higher Ed*, May 29, 2018. https://www.insidehighered.com/news/2018/05/29/rift-among-scholars-over-treatment-junot-d%C3%ADaz-he-faces-harassment-and-misconduct.

Genette, Gérard. *Paratexts: Thresholds of Interpretation*. Translated by Jane E. Lewin. Cambridge: Cambridge UP, 1997.

Goldberg, Emma. "Suitable for the Classroom? #MeToo Spurs a Rethinking." *The New York Times*, October 8, 2019.

Gyasi, Yaa. *Homegoing*. New York: Knopf, 2016.

Habash, Gale. "Just How Much Does a Pulitzer Prize Help a Book's Sales?" *Publishers Weekly*, April 19, 2012. https://www.publishersweekly.com/pw/by-topic/

industry-news/awards-and-prizes/article/51573-just-how-much-does-a-pulitzer-prize-help-a-book-s-sales.html.

Hassan, Waïl S. "World Literature in the Age of Globalization: Reflections on an Anthology." *College English* 63, no. 1 (September 2000): 38-47. https://doi.org/10.2307/379030.

Hayot, Eric. "Worlds, Literature, Systems." In *On Literary Worlds*, 30-42. Oxford: Oxford UP, 2012.

Kang, Han. *The Vegetarian*. London: Hogarth, 2016.

Khair, Tabish. "Death of the Reader." *OPEN Magazine*, October 2011. https://openthemagazine.com/essays/arts-letters/death-of-the-reader/.

Krotov, Mark and Dayna Tortorici. "'The Rest is Indeed Horseshit,' Pt. 6: On World Lit #BEEF." *n+1 Magazine* 23 (2013). Accessed August 15, 2020. https://nplusonemag.com/online-only/horseshit/the-rest-is-indeed-horseshit-pt-6/.

———. "World Lite: What is Global Literature?" *n+1 Magazine* 17 (Fall 2013). Accessed April 1, 2020. https://nplusonemag.com/issue-17/the-intellectual-situation/world-lite/.

McCormack, Leah. "Reclaiming Silenced and Erased Histories: The Paratextual Devices of Historic Metafiction." *Making Connections* 14, no. 2 (Fall 2013): 37-54.

McCoy, Beth A. "Race and the (Para)textual Condition." *PMLA: Special Topic: The History of the Book and the Idea of Literature* 121, no. 1 (January 2006): 156-169. https://www.jstor.org/stable/25486294.

Moretti, Franco. "Conjectures on World Literature." *New Left Review* 1 (January/February 2000): 54-68.

Mufti, Aamir R. "Orientalism and the Institution of World Literatures." *Critical Inquiry* 36 (2010): 458-493. https://doi.org/10.1086/653408.

Porter, Tom. "To Teach or Not to Teach? Nadia Celis on #MeToo and Junot Díaz." *Bowdoin*, October 14, 2019. https://www.bowdoin.edu/news/2019/10/to-teach-or-not-to-teach-nadia-celis-on-metoo-and-junot-d%C3%ADaz.html.

Rajaram, Poorva and Michael Griffith. "Why World Literature Looks Different in Brooklyn." *3 Quarks Daily* (blog). https://3quarksdaily.com/3quarksdaily/2013/08/why-world-literature-looks-different-from-brooklyn.html.

Robbins, Bruce. "Bad Atrocity Writing." *n+1 Magazine* 32 (2018). Accessed December 17, 2020. https://nplusonemag.com/issue-32/politics/bad-atrocity-writing/.

Said, Edward. "Humanism's Sphere." *Humanism and Democratic Criticism*, 1-30. New York: Columbia UP, 2004.

Singh, Amardeep. "On N+1's 'World Lite.'" *Electrostani* (blog), August 27, 2013. http://www.electrostani.com/2013/08/on-n1s-world-lite.html.

Solheim, Jennifer. "n+1's World Lite: A Hopeful Response." *Jennifer Solheim* (blog), August 17, 2013. https://jennifersolheim.com/2013/08/17/n1s-world-lite-a-hopeful-response/.

Strich, Fritz. *Goethe and World Literature*. Translated by C. A. M. Sym. London: Routledge & Kegan Paul Ltd., 1949.

Walkowitz, Rebecca. "Comparison Literature." *New Literary History* 40, no. 3 (Summer 2009): 567-582. https://www.jstor.org/stable/27760276.

Chapter 6

"The strange familiar:" coming home in and as an *Americanah*

Pritika Pradhan

Minnesota State University

Abstract

The return home in migrant narratives is viewed by critics such as Elleke Boehmer as the culmination of the migrant's journey. To come back to the supposedly unchanged homeland entails either a settling of migrant identity via a return to a static order, or of the entrapment and fragmentation of that identity under the dysfunctional, and usually neo-colonial, order that had precipitated departure. Such simplistic critiques—the legacy of postcolonial paradigms—are conceptually and imaginatively inadequate to engage with a more complex phenomenon of repatriation in the twenty-first century. Here migration is increasingly characterized by multidirectional movements between several nations, and its effects on migrant identity are further intensified—rather than settled—by return. In Chimamanda Ngozi Adichie's *Americanah* (2013), for instance, the traditional postcolonial model of journeying from the homeland to the metropolis and back is replaced with the interwoven movements of various characters between the homeland (Nigeria), the erstwhile colonial mother country (Britain), and the more recent aspirational metropolis (America). Further, the geopolitical designations of each place remain unstable, with the homeland representing an volatile, exhilarating order, both bustling and corrupt in the wake of skewed neo-liberal "reforms" that occur in the meantime of migration. For *Americanah's* repatriates, the return home thus represents a step further in the migration journey, in which identity is characterized by the coexistence of native belonging and alien self-consciousness, the terms of which must be constantly re-negotiated in order to approach personal, political and erotic modes of fulfillment.

Keywords: Adichie, Chimamanda Ngozi; Americanah; Migrant Narratives; Postcolonialism

***

Representations of migration in twenty-first-century literature have split the traditional binary of birthplace and destination, or postcolonial periphery and metropole, into a spectrum of nuanced and amorphous conceptions of movement and place. While migration in the works of mid to late twentieth-century writers such as V. S. Naipaul was characterized by what critic James Wood calls an "arrowlike terminality"—an irreversible journey from the homeland to the destination—contemporary advances in globalization, social mobility, and modes of travel have influenced a more intricate and fragmented form of migration narrative in the twenty-first century. These migration narratives, notably in the work of writers such as Amit Chaudhuri, Chimamanda Ngozi Adichie, and Yaa Gyasi, depict multidirectional journeys between several places whose geopolitical designations (such as metropole and periphery) are in flux.[1] This shift is particularly evident in representations of the migrant's return to the homeland. In postwar literature, return, when it featured at all, represented the cessation of the migrant's journey. Postcolonial critic Elleke Boehmer describes "homecoming" as the "culminating event in the journey narrative" that ends narrative possibilities for the migrant self, either through a reconnection with the past, or through entrapment in the dysfunctional neocolonial order that had precipitated departure in the first place.[2] However, in twenty-first-century literature, the homeland assumes some of the socio-economic and cultural dynamism previously associated with migrant destinations, so that return represents a further step in the migrant's trajectory, which intensifies the unsettling effects of migration on identity.

Chimamanda Ngozi Adichie's novel *Americanah* (2013) follows its protagonists, Ifemelu and Obinze, across three nations—the homeland of Nigeria; the former colonial mother country, Britain; and the current aspirational metropole, America—and then traces their repatriate trajectories in a Nigeria that

---

[1] For a discussion of the shift from irrevocable journeys to multidirectional movements in migration, and the associated fragmentation of narrative, see James Wood's review of Sunjeev Sahota's 2021 novel *China Room* in James Wood, "Sunjeev Sahota's Novels of Arrival and Departure," *The New Yorker*, August 2, 2021, https://www.newyorker.com/magazine/2021/08/09/sunjeev-sahotas-novels-of-arrival-and-departure. In addition to the works of Adichie and Sahota, other novels featuring multidirectional movements include Amit Chaudhuri's *Odysseus Abroad* (2015) and Yaa Gyasi's *Homegoing* (2016).

[2] Elleke Boehmer, *Colonial and Postcolonial Literature*, rev. ed. (Oxford: Oxford UP, 2005), 201.

represents an exhilarating order, bustling and corrupt, in the wake of neoliberal reforms implemented in the meantime of migration. Returning to this changing homeland blurs the distinctions the protagonists negotiate (home and away, foreign and familiar, citizen and alien), leading them to seek illusory pre-migratory ideals of belonging. The novel itself reflects their longing through its conventional romantic conclusion that aspires to, and yet problematizes, the pre-migratory order. As the implications of *Americanah*'s radical remapping of migration exceeds the bounds and desires of its romantic plot, the novel inadvertently reveals the ethical and aesthetic implications of excluding the homeland from discourses of migration—an exclusion that it both colludes in and attempts to redress by reconfiguring return as the extended afterlife of migration. Uncovering how *Americanah* at once fulfills and, more interestingly, fails its own cosmopolitan possibilities also indicates the way forward for subfields in contemporary literature, from "Global Anglophone" studies to Post45 studies, by recognizing and including the dynamism and diversity of the homeland left behind.

Americanah is particularly pertinent to the study of the return to a changing homeland because Adichie's depiction of a rapidly transforming and cosmopolitan twenty-first-century Nigeria converges with contemporary discourses on the fundamentally diverse, mobile, and transnational nature of African societies. In his influential formulation of "Afropolitanism," Cameroonian philosopher Achille Mbembe describes how the constant movement of Black and non-Black populations to, out of, and within Africa has shaped a continent characterized since pre-colonial times by "itinerancy, mobility, and displacement," of which the global present is an acceleration.[3] Mbembe effectively extends to the continent ideas of mobility and multiplicity that were initially accorded to the diaspora in earlier discourses of Afropolitanism. The term "Afropolitanism," a portmanteau of the words "African" and "cosmopolitanism," was first popularized by the novelist Taiye Selasi (of Nigerian and Ghanaian descent, born in London, and raised in Boston), in her essay "Bye-Bye Babar," to describe "the newest generation of African emigrants," whose parents had left Africa in the 1960-70s and who grew up moving between different global metropolises and institutions, negotiating African as well as non-African cultures. Selasi writes, "You'll know us by our funny blend of London fashion, New York jargon, African ethics, and academic successes. Some of us are ethnic mixes, e.g. Ghanaian and Canadian, Nigerian and Swiss; others merely cultural mutts: American accent, European

---

[3] Achille Mbembe, "Afropolitanism," in *Africa Remix: Contemporary Art of a Continent*, eds. Simon Njami and Lucy Durán (Johannesburg: Jacana, 2007), 27.

affect, African ethos."[4] While Selasi focuses on the diaspora, Mbembe asserts the essential cosmopolitanism of the African continent itself: "Our [African] way of belonging to the world, of being in the world and inhabiting it, has always been marked by, if not cultural mixing, then at least the interweaving of worlds."[5] What both Selasi's and Mbembe's articulations of Afropolitanism have in common is a conception of African identity based on an intermixture of cultural modes, so that any essentialist or monolithic understanding of African authenticity, including race-based movements such as pan-Africanism and *négritude*, becomes untenable.

Adichie, whose work has been appropriated by members of the Afropolitan diaspora, stands in a complicated relation to discourses of Afropolitanism.[6] While she is skeptical of the term itself, her description of Africa converges with the "Afropolitan" characterization of the African continent in terms of diversity and constant change:

> I am tired of this word [Afropolitan]. I am African... [H]istory (sadly not well known) shows that cosmopolitanism doesn't date from yesterday: many African kings from the West coast sent their children to study in Europe. And much later, the generation of my father traveled a lot, there have been numerous waves of people coming back in the 1960's, and who have not stopped moving. They define themselves as Africans.[7]

Even as she refutes the label, Adichie's statement, like Mbembe's formulation of Afropolitanism, affirms the essential cosmopolitanism of African societies and cultures *avant la lettre*. In asserting her African identity, Adichie upholds

---

[4] Taiye Selasi, "Bye-Bye Babar," *The Lip Magazine*, March 3, 2005, http://thelip.robertsharp.co.uk/?p=76.

[5] Mbembe, "Afropolitanism," 28.

[6] For instance, Serena Guarracino points out how the blog *The Afrolibrarians* identifies Adichie as "The Afropolitan Anthropologist," and how Adichie features on a Pinterest board titled "Stylish Afropolitan Woman." See Serena Guarracino, "Writing 'so raw and true': Blogging in Chimamanda Ngozi Adichie's *Americanah*," *Between* 4, no. 8 (November 2014): 11, https://doi.org.10.13125/2039-6597/1320.

[7] Chimamanda Ngozi Adichie, "Nigeria - Chimamanda Ngozi Adichie: 'Africaine oui, Afropolitaine, sûrement pas,'" interview by Valérie Marin La Meslée, *Le Point Afrique*, February 5, 2015, https://www.lepoint.fr/culture/nigeria-chimamanda-ngozi-adichie-africaine-oui-afropolitaine-surement-pas-05-02-2015-1902573_3.php. Translation done by Stephanie Bosch Santana, "Exorcizing the future: Afropolitanism's spectral origins," *Journal of African Cultural Studies* 28, no. 1 (March 2016): 121-122, https://www.jstor.org/stable/24758438.

an identity that has centuries of cultural interfusion and exchange at its core, even as she stands by its singularity and authenticity.

In *Americanah*, the complicated cosmopolitanism of African identity is encapsulated by the novel's title itself, an English loanword used by Nigerians at home to denote the exaggerated American personas sometimes adopted by America-returned Nigerian expatriates. Adichie describes "Americanah" as "a kind of playful word that's used for people who have been to the U.S. and who come back to Nigeria with American affectations, or... pretend that they no longer understand Igbo or Yoruba or Hausa."[8] Her linguistically aware explanation casts the term "Americanah" as an act of gentle mockery, where the America-returned repatriate is labeled by an English word refracted through the Nigerian languages she pretends to no longer understand. This usage of the term exemplifies what Simon Gikandi describes as the "provincialization" of English, where English is deprived of "the ecumenical status of the global" by recognizing it as part of "the diversity and plurality of world languages," with "many varieties, each with multiple registers."[9] Gikandi's formulation of provincialization enacts cosmopolitanism at the ground level, where African multiplicity is realized as lived experience. At the same time, "Americanah" challenges Anglophone normativity: as the title of an English-language novel published in the United States, it compels American readers to perceive their own nomenclature made alien through the addition of the suffix -*ah*. Mbembe characterizes Afropolitanism as the "the ability to recognise [sic] one's face in that of a foreigner... to domesticate the unfamiliar, to work with what seem to be opposites."[10] In compelling Nigerian and American readers alike to recognize the otherness in themselves, "Americanah" exemplifies the entwined promise of cosmopolitanism and provincialization, where the Western metropole is revealed as one province among many, and the supposedly peripheral province becomes a polis that encompasses the changing world.

The promises of the novel's cosmopolitan-provincialized title find their realization in its plot. Instead of ending with Ifemelu's return, *Americanah* opens with the anticipation of her return, drawing it out over several chapters that chronicle intersecting journeys between Nigeria, Britain, and the United States, thereby questioning the binary between beginning and end, past and present, departure and return. The postcolonial linear model of migration from

[8] Chimamanda Ngozi Adichie, "'Americanah' Author Explains 'Learning' To Be Black in In The U.S.," interview by David Bianculli, NPR, June 27, 2013, https://www.npr.org/transcripts/195598496.

[9] Simon Gikandi, "Editor's Column: Provincializing English," *PMLA* 129, no. 1 (January 2014): 13, https://www.jstor.org/stable/24769418.

[10] Mbembe, "Afropolitanism," 28.

the homeland to the metropolis and back is no longer viable in a world of ambiguous movement between spaces of shifting geopolitical import, where America is displacing the erstwhile mother country of Britain as the aspirational metropolis, and contemporary Nigeria combines characteristics of home and migrant destination. Return to this changing homeland, where characters experience simultaneous belonging and alienation, becomes a complicated continuation of migration that unravels the coordinates of departure and return, periphery and metropole that are used to employ migration.

However, if *Americanah* posits returning to a heterogeneous homeland as an unraveling of the linear migratory ideal, its depiction of events following that return can be read as a mode of cheating on its own innovation. The reunion of Ifemelu with Obinze (who is married at the time of her return) literalizes the novel's struggle to contain the consequences of its revised trajectory by trying to revert to a prelapsarian, pre-migration past. In its abrupt and clumsy commitment to a conventional marriage plot, which is actually a re-marriage plot, *Americanah* unwittingly reveals the problematic focus of migration narratives on the experiences of the migrant individual abroad at the cost of entities at home—past lovers, families, the nation—that undergo their own transformation while the migrant is abroad, and may not be amenable to the returning migrant's desire for uncontested belonging. In this essay, I will discuss the implications of the homeland as the overlooked remainder of migration in the context of Kosi, Obinze's wife, whose abandonment signifies the failure of this very cosmopolitan novel to formulate a truly cosmopolitan ethics that allows for the coexistence of diverse and dissonant perspectives at home. *Americanah*'s awkward selective exclusion of the homeland paradoxically suggests a way to include and diversify representations of the homeland in the study of postcolonial, Post45, and Global Anglophone literature, which have similarly excluded the migrant's homeland in order to focus on the migrant's journey. Ironically, the enduring value of *Americanah* as a work of migration literature—and as a focus for contemporary literature studies—may lie in the lives it leaves behind in its enactments of migration, and in the stories it does not tell.

The home and the world

The fluidity of movement in *Americanah* enacts the ambiguity in the etymology of the term "migration" itself: the Latin *migrare* ("to wander" or "to move") is aimless and ambiguous, so that going away from one place is also coming to another place. In geopolitical terms, however, migration has been viewed as a largely postcolonial phenomenon, with the migrant seeking to escape from his or her "Third World" nation and former colony, often to the former mother country. Elleke Boehmer writes of migrant literatures as "represent[ing] a geographic, cultural, and political retreat by writers from the new but ailing nations of the postcolonial world back to the old metropolis," a characterization that configures migration in terms of a linearity that is both spatial and temporal. This linearity lends itself to being narrativized as an unambiguous departure to a dynamic life that is conducive to the formation of narrative, with return being equated with stagnation.[11]

However, the journeys in *Americanah* defy linearity by challenging the conventional aspirational trajectory of migration. The novel opens with Ifemelu's decision to return to Nigeria, which upsets both the aspirational trajectory of migration and also its causality. By her own admission, Ifemelu has no "cause" to return, for hers is a successful migrant story: she is a celebrated blogger with a Fellowship at Princeton and is in a stable romantic relationship. Instead, her rationale for returning is emotional rather than economic: she wishes to come home, where her "sense of belonging is least contested," as Adichie writes of her own decision to return to Nigeria.[12] In its reversal of the conventional migrant trajectory, Ifemelu's decision is in keeping with the "refus[al] on principle of any form of victim identity" that Achille Mbembe identifies as essential to Afropolitanism.[13] Miriam Pahl, expanding on Mbembe's formulation, argues that he envisages "more nuanced and differentiated subject positions that Afropolitans inhabit" by refusing the "oppositional, victimized position that 'Africa' is conventionally assigned."[14] A nuanced understanding of migrant experiences and affects also calls for a new kind of narrative that does not submit to easy chains of causality or direction.

Such a nuanced portrayal is evident in the representation of Ifemelu's longing to return home, described by the narrator in formless, cumulative terms that do not point to any specific cause, and thus defy easy narrativization: "[T]here was cement in her soul… an early morning disease of fatigue, a bleakness and borderlessness. It brought with it amorphous longings, shapeless desires, brief imaginary glints of other lives she could be living, that over the months melded into a piercing homesickness."[15] The terms used to evoke Ifemelu's homesickness enact the amorphousness they describe, a layered accumulation of gradations

---

[11] Boehmer, *Colonial and Postcolonial Literature*, 238.

[12] Chimamanda Ngozi Adichie, "Buildings fall down, pensions aren't paid, politicians are murdered, riots are in the air … and yet I love Nigeria," *The Guardian*, August 7, 2006, http://www.theguardian.com/commentisfree/2006/aug/08/comment.features11.

[13] Mbembe, "Afropolitanism," 28-29.

[14] Miriam Pahl, "Afropolitanism as critical consciousness: Chimamanda Ngozi Adichie's and Teju Cole's internet presence," *Journal of African Cultural Studies* 28, no. 1 (March 2016), 76, https://www.jstor.org/stable/24758432.

[15] Chimamanda Ngozi Adichie, *Americanah* (New York: Knopf, 2013), 7.

of feeling that elude analysis. Her formless and causeless inner motivations signify the non-linear nature of her migration trajectory.

Fittingly, Ifemelu's homesickness is nurtured over the amorphous medium of the Internet. By enabling the construction and diffusion of identities and the formation of imaginary communities, the Internet is both cause and symptom of a melding world. Søren Frank writes that the Internet "mak[es] traveling and communication possible on a scale previously unimaginable [so that] the world is accelerating and contracting at one and the same time; material and immaterial borders are blurring and becoming permeable."[16] At the same time, however, Ifemelu's engagement with the Internet also encapsulates the unconscious ironies that underlie her homesickness. Her very longing to return home, where her "belonging is least contested," is nourished through looking at images of a rapidly changing Nigeria:

> [E]ach click brought yet another story of a young person who had recently moved back home, clothed in American or British degrees, to start an investment company, a music production business... She looked at photographs of these men and women and felt the dull ache of loss, as though they had prised open her hand and taken something of hers. They were living her life.[17]

Even as Nigeria signifies to her an ideal of stability and belonging, she locates this ideal in images of young Nigerian repatriates—members of the Afropolitan diaspora described by Selasi—who exemplify mobility and change.

This fluidity of the Internet both enacts and enables the mobility of Afropolitan communities at home and abroad. Mbembe, in an interview titled "The Internet is Afropolitan," argues that the Internet's state of "permanent transformation, mutation, conversion and circulation" is an "essential dimension of what we can call African culture," thus making it particularly suited to the continent's Afropolitan past and present.[18] As Pahl points out, the converse is equally true: the term and discourses of Afropolitanism (such as Selasi's essay as well as Mbembe's interview) find an outlet and readership through the Internet.[19] In the United States, Ifemelu herself is a producer of online

---

[16] Søren Frank, *Migration and Literature: Günter Grass, Milan Kundera, Salman Rushdie, and Jan Kjærstad* (New York: Palgrave Macmillan, 1998), 2.

[17] Adichie, *Americanah*, 7.

[18] Achille Mbembe, "The Internet Is Afropolitan," interview by Bregtje van der Haak, *The Chimurenga Chronic New Cartographies*, August 7, 2015, http://chimurengachronic.co.za/the internet-is-afropolitan/.

[19] Pahl, "Afropolitanism as critical consciousness," 77.

Afropolitan discourse (despite Adichie's abjuration of the term) through her successful blog on race as a global phenomenon that affects not only "American Blacks," but also "Non-American Blacks" such as herself. As she remarks wryly, "I only became black when I came to America."[20] Her alienation in America, where she is classified as "black" despite not sharing the same cultural experiences as African Americans, is certainly one of the contributors to her homesickness. That her desire for uncontested belonging is nurtured online, through images of rapid and complex change displayed in a changing medium, renders her desire ironic and presages the disorientations she experiences on returning to a changing homeland.

Ifemelu's return to Nigeria is rendered ambivalent by the country's transformation from the homeland of her memory and desire into a dizzying hub of commerce. She is unsettled by her homeland on her return, by the ubiquity of cellphones and billboards: "At first, Lagos assaulted her... Commerce thrummed too defiantly."[21] Lagos' brash new commercial ways make her not only see the city anew, but also reexamine her past: "Had it always been like this or had it changed so much in her absence?"[22] Feeling disoriented by an unfamiliar homeland where she had expected to experience uncomplicated belonging, she experiences a vertiginous uncanniness, "the dizzying sensation of falling, falling into the new person she had become, falling into the strange familiar."[23]

Ironically, the very changes that disorient Ifemelu enable her successful return, since they reflect how Nigeria has become a place not unlike England or America, where migrants can settle without suffering stasis and diminishment: a place where migrant stories and opportunities lie. Her friend Ranyinudo claims: "Lagos is now full of American returnees, so you better come back and join them."[24] The reappointment of the homeland as an exciting migrant destination overturns conventional formulations of the homeland as the remainder of migration, necessarily left behind so that the migrant can move. As a homeland that its protagonists can return to without undergoing stasis or despair, Nigeria becomes what desired migrant destinations such as Britain and the United States represent in the scheme of migration literature: a rapidly changing space that enables reinventions of migrant identity. Returning migrants

---

[20] Adichie, *Americanah*, 359.

[21] Adichie, *Americanah*, 475.

[22] Adichie, *Americanah*, 475.

[23] Adichie, *Americanah*, 475.

[24] Adichie, *Americanah*, 16.

become successful repatriates, members of the Afropolitan elite whom Ifemelu both envies and finds herself reluctantly joining on her return.

Ifemelu's ambivalence towards her changing homeland is reflected in her equivocal attitude towards her own status as an "Americanah." She is designated as such by her friend Ranyinudo when she voices her dismay at the complexities of modern Nigerian life. She ironically first feels at home in the Nigerpolitan Club for repatriates from America and England, where she discovers a longing for the America she left behind, even as she is uncomfortable with their more exaggerated affectations, their sense of America-returned superiority, which she satirizes in a new blog. Neither entirely Lagosian nor wholly Americanah, she only experiences true homecoming when she reunites with Obinze, "her first love, her first lover, the only person with whom she had never felt the need to explain herself."[25]

Yet returning to Obinze does not signify belonging, but rather shows how Ifemelu is implicated in the perplexing transformations and exchanges of modern Nigerian life. During her stay in America from the early 1990s until 2008, Nigeria morphed into a socio-economically dynamic, or "hustling" (to use the novel's term), entity, under President Olusegun Obasanjo's neoliberal economic reforms. Oil revenues and the free entry of foreign investment resulted in the dizzying, and often dubious, enrichment of the Nigerian middle and upper classes. This rise is exemplified by Obinze's trajectory: following his deportation from England as an illegal immigrant, he acquires the patronage of "Chief," a shady businessman with political connections, and suddenly becomes a wealthy "evaluation consult[ant]," a real estate agent catering to foreign companies in Nigeria. Adichie dwells on the bright, tinselly gilding of Obinze's milieu with bluntness and ambivalence: while he makes a dizzying ascent up the social scale of Lagos, his sudden wealth makes him experience "a disorienting strangeness because his mind had not changed at the same pace as his life."[26] In this scenario, the narrative frames his reunion with Ifemelu as a return to the honesty and authenticity that distinguished their relationship.

Ifemelu and Obinze's initial union, and later reunion, as repatriates is portrayed as a meeting of soulmates who bonded over a shared alienation from their world, a shared longing for honesty and forthrightness. Their alienation originates in their particular experiences at home, and makes them to some extent aliens in their own land, long before they migrate. Obinze does not fit into the patriarchal norms of Nigerian Igbo masculinity, having been raised by his widowed mother, and having learnt from her his unmasculine penchant for

---

[25] Adichie, *Americanah*, 7.

[26] Adichie, *Americanah*, 33.

reading and cooking. He is attracted to Ifemelu because of her independence of mind, manifested in her defiance of gender expectations: "Other girls would have pretended that they had never let another boy touch them, but not her, never her. There was a vivid honesty about her."[27] Ifemelu is herself estranged from the norms of traditional Nigerian femininity, which include the hypocritical piety modeled by her mother, "a person who had to spread the cloak of religion over her own petty desires."[28] She also objects to the prevalent Nigerian ideal of female beauty, which requires naturally "kinky" African hair to be subjected to damaging relaxers and imported weaves.[29] Obinze and Ifemelu's alienation, which reveals how the norms and ideals of the homeland already incorporate foreign imports, from Christianity to standards of female beauty, enhances the irony of their desire for pre-migration belonging.

If Nigeria as the homeland undermines the divide between the foreign and the familiar, the "West" that Nigerians long for is also changing and unstable. We see the effects of changing definitions of the West play out across successive generations of Nigerian families. For Ifemelu's and Obinze's parents, who would have witnessed the British colonial regime that ended in 1960, the West is Britain, the mother country and the migrant destination of choice. By the protagonists' adolescence in the 1980s, however, America emerged as the new desirable metropole, having displaced Britain as the preeminent world power. Obinze's mother, a London-educated professor of literature, complains that he is "besotted with America," to which he replies: "America is the future."[30] His words reveal the shift of power between nations as observed by an ambitious "Third World" migrant from a former colony who is determined to select the best prospect. By emphasizing America as the present (during the 80s), and Britain as the past of migration, the novel destabilizes the idea of a fixed destination abroad and paves the way for the homeland to emerge as the next desirable destination.

Americanah also positions the homeland as a destination by critiquing the appeal of migrant destinations abroad, where the protagonists undergo traumas of obstructed arrival and unsuccessful integration. Obinze, who had so confidently believed in America, is denied a visa following the September 11

---

[27] Adichie, *Americanah*, 24.

[28] Adichie, *Americanah*, 63.

[29] "Kinky" is one of the adjectives prominently used by Adichie's narrator and her protagonist Ifemelu to describe Ifemelu's hair (Adichie, *Americanah*, 12, 250, 252, 258). Specifically, "natural [African/African American] hair" types are described as "coarse, oily, kinky, or curly" (357). In using this word, I seek to preserve the author's and the character's original word choice.

[30] Adichie, *Americanah*, 84.

attacks. He ends up in England as an impoverished illegal migrant, only to be deported—or, to use the official term, "removed... like a thing without breath or mind."[31] While Ifemelu has an outwardly successful stay in America, she experiences the underlying racial tensions of a supposedly multicultural society by being marked out as "black" and classified with African Americans, despite not having experienced the same shared history of racial discrimination in Nigeria. Paradoxically, Ifemelu's experiences of classification and discrimination in America bring her closer to her homeland by leading her to embrace her identity as a Nigerian Igbo woman with naturally kinky hair in a way she had not felt free to do in Nigeria. Her romantic trajectory in America also anticipates her eventual return. Though she forms promising relationships—first with a wealthy white American businessman, and then a deeper bond with an African American academic—she finds them ultimately unsatisfying, for her partners neither share nor comprehend her particular experience as a non-American Black woman in America. Romantic fulfillment for Ifemelu is possible only with Obinze, her first and future love, and a Nigerian Igbo returnee like herself.

Ifemelu and Obinze's reunion reveals the novel's problematic underlying commitment to linearity beneath its non-linear structure. The novel's cycles of repetition and return add up to a tale of *bildung*, or coming of age, which culminates when Ifemelu returns to her place of imagined belonging: home with Obinze, home in Nigeria. Yet this return requires that the protagonist, and the narrative itself, discount the changes that have happened in the homeland when she was away. These changes are embodied in the figure of Kosi, Obinze's wife, whom he leaves in order to reunite with Ifemelu.

Belonging

The transformed Nigeria that disorients Ifemelu on her return has an emotional and erotic dimension, represented by the marriage of Obinze and Kosi during Ifemelu's stay in America. Ifemelu's return fractures the idea of home: if Obinze reunites with Ifemelu, who is depicted as his soulmate and spiritual home, where does that leave his marital home he built with Kosi in her absence? The novel "resolves" this rupture through a conventional romantic ending for Ifemelu and Obinze, which coincides roughly with Ifemelu's "resolution" of finally feeling at home in a changed Nigeria. In the process, however, *Americanah* withdraws from the implications of its sophisticated rewriting of migration and repatriation to a changing homeland, instead mirroring its protagonist's desire to return to a pre-migration sense of belonging.

---

[31] Adichie, *Americanah*, 345.

To "justify" Ifemelu and Obinze's reunion, the narrative dismisses Kosi as the embodiment of a home that never was: a typically conservative, close-minded, and thoroughly domestic Nigerian woman who cannot fulfill Obinze's emotional and intellectual needs. As he explains to Ifemelu: "She has really basic, mainstream ideas of what a wife should be... There's a lot of pretending in my marriage." [32] Obinze's characterization aligns Kosi with the repressive gender norms and social hypocrisies that both he and Ifemelu find suffocating. Kosi's dismissal, even demonization, enables the novel to portray Obinze and Ifemelu's reunion as a migration that is also a true homecoming: Obinze, the mobile male migrant, leaves his uninteresting wife for the outspoken and progressive Ifemelu, a prospect more attractive to him—and, not incidentally, to the novel's Western and Westernized, English-speaking readers.

In creating a binary between Kosi as the deserted homeland and Ifemelu as the cosmopolitan object of desire, the novel privileges a specific kind of Western-educated, liberal-minded African subjectivity, which converges with the sophisticated intellectual sensibilities of the Afropolitan diaspora. Taiye Selasi describes how later generations of the Afropolitan diaspora work in creative fields such as "media, politics, music, venture capital, design," as opposed to the "traditional professions like doctoring, lawyering, banking, engineering" pursued by their parents, thereby choosing to be producers of cultural and political discourse. [33] Ifemelu also pursues this path as a blogger, creating compelling critical narratives about America's racial inequality from a foreigner's point of view and later writing about the inequities of modern Nigerian society from her perspective as a repatriate. The contrast between Ifemelu's passionate public expressiveness and Kosi's relative silence reveals how diasporic voices at home and abroad risk drowning out the perspectives of those left behind: those who lack the privileges and access of the diaspora. Kenyan writer Binyavanga Wainaina criticizes diaspora-centric understandings of Afropolitanism as formulated by and for a privileged "Black African [diasporic] elite" who can afford to circulate in Western metropolises with ease. [34] Afropolitan discourses that focus on the diaspora abroad and repatriates at home, at the cost of the perspectives of Africans resident in Africa, risk perpetuating the exclusion of the homeland from migration narratives. The selective erasure of aspects of the modern homeland that are not in sync with diasporic Afropolitan sensibilities is dramatized in the case of Kosi, who is configured as representative of the stagnant, deserted homeland of repressive

---

[32] Adichie, *Americanah*, 555.

[33] Selasi, "Bye-Bye Babar."

[34] Gemma Solés, "Wainaina on Afropolitanism," *UrbanAfrica.Net*, April 4, 2014, http://www. urbanafrica.net/urban-voices/wainaina-afropolitanism/.

gender norms, religious fundamentalism, and social backwardness. In discursive terms, Kosi is aligned with what Simon Gikandi terms "the malady of Afro-pessimism:" the "belief that the continent and its populace is hopelessly imprisoned in its past, trapped [in] a vicious circle of underdevelopment, and held hostage to corrupt institutions" for which Afropolitanism offers a "hermeneutics of redemption."[35] In other words, Kosi becomes the stagnant homeland to which Ifemelu, the mobile, progressive, and modern Afropolitan, is both contrast and corrective.

At the same time, the narrative's configuration of Kosi as the static homeland suppresses the ways in which she is as much an aspect of Nigerian modernity as is Ifemelu with her outspoken progressiveness, or Obinze with his critical complicity. A narrative flashback reveals how Obinze had himself associated Kosi with his newly rich and strange life: "He was also newly rich and newly disoriented... Kosi became a touchstone of realness. If he could be with her, so extraordinarily beautiful and yet so ordinary, predictable and domestic and dedicated, then perhaps his life would start to seem believably his."[36] Obinze's imaginings reduce Kosi to a desirable asset for his new lifestyle, at once trophy and anchor. Having acquired her, and having settled into the life of material comfort he sought in Nigeria since his deportation from England, he tires of its certainties and hypocrisies in which he is implicated. In leaving Kosi, he seeks to leave behind aspects of the "Afro-pessimistic" homeland of corrupt institutions of which he feels ashamed, even as he benefits from them materially.

Serena Guarracino frames Obinze and Ifemelu's reunion as signifying the presence of "the Nigeria of Chiefs and locally-based businessmen alongside that of intellectual migrants with foreign PhDs" in a "dialogue" that enables the generation of a new Nigerian identity.[37] This reading assumes that the two Nigerias represented by Obinze and Ifemelu—a corrupt and deeply unequal society and a progressive cosmopolitan order respectively—are mutually exclusive. However, the "good" and "bad" visions of modern Nigeria are mutually implicated, as seen in the case of Kosi. If Kosi's presence signifies Obinze's implication in the corruption and inequality of modern Nigeria, her erasure reveals Ifemelu's complicity in the same following her repatriation. Despite seeking a pre-migration sense of belonging, Ifemelu returns as a repatriate in a position of relative privilege: an American citizen, cushioned by American money and connections that ironically facilitate her fantasy of belonging. Her geographical

---

[35] Simon Gikandi, "Preface," in *Negotiating Afropolitanism: Essays on Borders and Spaces in Contemporary African Literature and Folklore*, eds. Jennifer Wawrizinek and J. K. S. Makokha (Amsterdam and New York: Rodopi, 2011), 9.

[36] Adichie, *Americanah*, 565.

[37] Guarracino, "Writing 'so raw and true,'" 21.

mobility—her choice to return to Nigeria, with the option to go back to America should her return not work out—is facilitated by her American citizenship, a fact mentioned by her father but not explored in the narrative. Similarly, her choice to rent an apartment in Ikoyi, the most affluent area in Lagos and the aspirational neighborhood of her childhood, is made possible by her considerable American earnings, as is her decision to leave her unfulfilling job at a Nigerian magazine to start a new blog on her life in Lagos. Tellingly, she selects for her blog's masthead "a dreamy photograph of an abandoned colonial house" facing her apartment.[38] Such an image shows that Ifemelu's post-repatriation trajectory is not unlike that of an occupying power: the Afropolitan repatriate has displaced the colonial mother country as well as the more recent aspirational metropole of America, to take over the homeland. Her reunion with Obinze fulfills the proprietary attitude of the repatriate towards the homeland, at the cost of erasing the perspective of the Nigerians left at home, represented by Kosi.

The reductive configuration of Kosi as the deserted homeland also reveals the disconcerting expedience of the novel's vision, which relentlessly sides with its migrant protagonists against alternate perspectives, specifically of those left behind at home. Abroad, Ifemelu and Obinze employ their ironic self-consciousness as outsiders to analyze the failings of other individuals and societies—the disapproving Republican family of Ifemelu's wealthy white boyfriend, a smug former classmate of Obinze's who settles in England and sees himself as British—while rarely subjecting themselves to that same gaze. In her blog in America, Ifemelu consciously assumes the position of an observant outsider, a "Non-American Black," to uncover the racism and xenophobia that have long ossified into habit for white Americans. However, following her return, Ifemelu's self-aware watchfulness is vitiated: she is no longer an outsider, but a relatively privileged repatriate whose resettlement entails the disruption of the home of a woman who does not have the attractions or benefits of a cosmopolitan life. The narrative reflects this lack of awareness by largely denying Kosi, and other characters like her, their own consciousness and perception. Kosi is seen mainly from Obinze's point of view before vanishing entirely from the narrative: shortly after a stand-off over Obinze's desire for a divorce, he abruptly turns up at Ifemelu's doorstep, stating: "Kosi is a good woman and my marriage was a kind of floating-along contentment, but I should never have married her."[39] The novel's relentless privileging of its migrant protagonists' perspectives indicates both an ethical poverty and a poverty of the imagination: a lack of awareness of the protagonists' implication

---

[38] Adichie, *Americanah*, 519.

[39] Adichie, *Americanah*, 588.

in the unequal networks of economic and erotic capital that they deplore. The narrative's failure to fully acknowledge the cost of their love for those left behind is also the novel's failure to fulfill its promise of a dynamic homeland: in Kosi, *Americanah* creates its own neglected remainder of migration, abandoned so that the protagonists can move on.

Ironically, we find the seeds of such dynamism in Adichie's viral TED talk, "The Danger of a Single Story" (2009), where she cautions against defining Africa as "a single story of catastrophe" that excites "patronizing, well-meaning pity" instead of the "possibility of a connection as human equals."[40] As Serena Guarracino points out, Adichie's lecture is "distinctly Afropolitan" for challenging the monolithic representation of Africa as a single story of stagnation and disaster.[41] Yet Adichie's unwavering privileging in *Americanah* of her repatriate protagonists' perspectives at the cost of the Nigerian women left behind enacts the danger she describes: the "single story" the novel relates of Kosi is effectively designed to "justify" her dispossession and desertion by her husband. Ifemelu's critical acumen as a blogger illustrates the intellectual power Afropolitans wield as producers of discourse; in fulfillment of Adichie's directive to avoid telling a "single story," she uses her blog to recognize and articulate overlooked "Non-American Black" perspectives that enrich the conversation on race in America. In contrast, Kosi is doubly a subaltern who cannot speak, for all her wealth and social position as Obinze's wife. She is abandoned not only by Obinze, but also by the narrative, which rarely recognizes her perspective or gives space to her interiority. In erasing Kosi, *Americanah* repeats the failure of conventional migration narratives to formulate an ethical and aesthetic vision in keeping with their sophisticated mapping of spatial journeys.

Conclusion

Will migration narratives necessarily create a remainder that is left behind by the mobile migrant? One does not need to speculate on alternate endings in order to hope for a migration narrative to be ethically and aesthetically responsive to the implications of its sophisticated remapping of migration and repatriation. Such responsiveness can be manifested in the narrative itself, by making space for the interiority of those left behind, whose lives are affected by the returning migrants' desires and actions. Discourses of cosmopolitanism and Afropolitanism offer fertile grounds for this narrative awareness. Kwame

---

[40] Chimamanda Ngozi Adichie (2009), *The Danger of a Single Story*, filmed in Oxford, TEDGlobal video, 18:34, https://www.ted.com/talks/chimamanda_ngozi_adichie_the_danger_of_a_single_story.

[41] Guarracino, "Writing 'so raw and true,'" 10.

Anthony Appiah's concept of cosmopolitan patriotism, where "everyone is... attached to a home of one's own, with its own cultural particularities, but taking pleasure from the presence of other, different places that are home to other, different people," is relevant to the ethics and aesthetics of migration narratives such as *Americanah*.[42] This is so not only because of the migrant's movement in multiple cultures, but also because the homeland itself is revealed to be a dynamic and diverse entity, undergoing continuous transformations before, during, and after the migrant's departure and return. In ethical terms, cosmopolitanism entails that individuals and communities take comfort and pride in their allegiance to their values, while also having the confidence and self-awareness to acknowledge that others will have their own cherished values, though these may be at variance with their own. In a more fully realized cosmopolitan narrative, even relatively unexciting characters such as Kosi could be afforded their own consciousness, creating a contrapuntal "atonal ensemble," to borrow Edward Said's term: an ensemble of "competitive and contradictory" perspectives and strands of discourse, without privileging one over the other.[43] Contrapuntal and cosmopolitan literatures of migration would further destabilize the cultural hegemony of the First World over the Third World by affirming the idea of a dynamic homeland with divergent voices.

Americanah's marginalized voices already contain the seeds of such creative divergence. In her confrontation with Obinze, Kosi protests incisively (if inelegantly) that he is breaking up their home in an attempt to erase the years separating him from a pre-migration ideal of romance and belonging: "I am a good wife. We have a marriage. Do you think you can just destroy this family... because your old girlfriend came back from America? Because you have had acrobatic sex that reminded you of your time in university?"[44] This compelling outburst is unusual in that it affords a glimpse into Kosi's inner life: while Obinze was characterizing Kosi as a dull, conventional woman to Ifemelu, she had been aware of his affair the entire time. Yet we only see this episode from Obinze's point of view: "Obinze backed away... He loathed Kosi, for knowing all this time and pretending she didn't know, and for the sludge of humiliation it

---

[42] Kwame Anthony Appiah, "Cosmopolitan Patriots," *Critical Inquiry* 23, no. 3 (Spring 1997): 618, https://www.jstor.org/10.1111/hic3.12362.

[43] Edward Said, *Culture and Imperialism* (New York: Knopf, 1993), 318; Edward Said, "The *Connection* Interview with Edward Said," interview by Christopher Lydon, *Interviews with Edward Said*, eds. Amritjit Singh and Bruce G. Johnson (Jackson: University of Mississippi Press, 2000), 202.

[44] Adichie, *Americanah*, 572.

left in his stomach."[45] Obinze's realization recasts Kosi's carefully cultivated appearance of conventionality and normality in another light: the actions of a pragmatic woman who knows that her husband, like many other wealthy men in Lagos, is likely to cheat on her, and who is nevertheless determined to assert her identity and dignity in the face of his disrespect and disdain. For a moment, we get a glimpse of another narrative, this time from Kosi's perspective, which reveals the conservative, often comic, habits that earn Obinze's disdain, such as attending a church with a "prayer service for Keeping Your Husband." These actions are driven by her fear of losing Obinze to another, more alluring woman—a fear that is, in her eyes, justified by the course of events. Such alternate perspectives as Kosi's are only hinted at rather than explored by the narrative. Yet their effect can be felt in the very act of erasure: the suddenness with which Kosi simply vanishes from the narrative indicates an awkwardness in reconciling her erasure with the protagonists' romantic reunion. The novel itself ends with Obinze turning up on Ifemelu's doorstep to commit to her, and Ifemelu inviting him inside, instead of, for instance, portraying their new life together. Despite its blinding movements and its dizzying rewriting of migration trajectories, *Americanah* shows a final hesitation to consummate a reunion it does so much to vindicate.

Through this admittedly counterintuitive analysis of a marginalized outburst, I hope to show how the contrapuntal reading of seemingly peripheral elements can enrich and diversify the dominant tendencies of the text, thereby deconstructing the divide between narrative periphery and center. Contrapuntal readings are particularly relevant to the field of contemporary literature, whose global shifts are manifested in the rise of new subfields, such as Post45 studies, as well as the expansion of existing categories (from "postcolonial" to "Global Anglophone"). Such expansions have produced understandable concerns about the disingenuous depoliticization of the field and the "re-centering [of] canonical writers and texts."[46] However, such depoliticization could be avoided if we employ contrapuntal readings to reveal how a supposed central norm, a text, a subfield, or a critical category, is itself constituted by cultural exchanges and the interfusion of ideas. This awareness is articulated by Adichie and other contemporary African writers like Teju Cole, who challenges his label as an "African writer" by aspiring towards multiple geographies: "'African, African-American, American-African, Black American, Nigerian American, Nigerian, American, Yoruba... My writing has European antecedents, Indian influences,

---

[45] Adichie, *Americanah*, 572.

[46] Yogita Goyal, "Postcolonialism, Still," *Post45* (*Forms of the Global Anglophone*), February 22, 2019, https://post45.org/2019/02/postcolonial-still/.

Icelandic fantasies, Brazilian aspirations.'"[47] Cole's assertion effectively updates Adichie's affirmation of African cosmopolitanism *avant la lettre*. To read the works of such authors requires expanding the conception of African literature to encompass the literature of nations outside Africa, while also uncovering African connections and influences in those literatures, thereby "recognis[ing] one's face in that of a foreigner," as Mbembe writes. The dissolution of disciplinary boundaries enacts the dissolution of geopolitical borders: in critical terms, Mbembe's conception of a cosmopolitan Africa not only dismantles the traditional postcolonial divide between the metropole and the postcolonial periphery, but also reveals the periphery itself to comprise an overlooked hinterland of diverse and divergent voices. As we navigate the increasingly global turn of contemporary studies and its subfields (postcolonial, Global Anglophone, Post45), we could keep in mind the model of a fluid and cosmopolitan hinterland: an overarching body of discourse is that not the stagnant remainder of mobility and multiplicity, but their utmost realization.

Works cited

Adichie, Chimamanda Ngozi. *Americanah*. New York: Knopf, 2013.

———. "'Americanah' Author Explains 'Learning' To Be Black in In The U.S." Interview by David Bianculli. NPR, June 27, 2013. https://www.npr.org/transcripts/195598496.

———. "Buildings fall down, pensions aren't paid, politicians are murdered, riots are in the air ... and yet I love Nigeria." *The Guardian*, August 7, 2006. http://www.theguardian.com/commentisfree/2006/aug/08/comment.features11.

———. (2009). *The Danger of a Single Story*. Filmed in Oxford. TEDGlobal video, 18:34. https://www.ted.com/talks/chimamanda_ngozi_adichie_the_danger_of_a_single_story.

———. "Nigeria - Chimamanda Ngozi Adichie: 'Africaine oui, Afropolitaine, sûrement pas." Interview by Valérie Marin La Meslée. *Le Point Afrique*, February, 5 2015. https://www.lepoint.fr/culture/nigeria-chimamanda-ngozi-adichie-africaine-oui-afropolitaine-surement-pas-05-02-2015-1902573_3.php.

Appiah, Kwame Anthony. "Cosmopolitan Patriots." *Critical Inquiry* 23, no. 3 (Spring 1997): 617-639. https://www.jstor.org/stable/1344038.

Boehmer, Elleke. *Colonial and Postcolonial Literature*. Rev. ed. Oxford: Oxford UP, 2005.

Cole, Teju. "Interview: Teju Cole." Interview by Aaron Bady. *African Writers in a New World, Post45.org*, January 19, 2015. https://post45.org/2015/01/interview-teju-cole/.

---

[47] Teju Cole, "Interview: Teju Cole," interview by Aaron Bady, *African Writers in a New World, Post45.org*, January 19, 2015, https://post45.org/2015/01/interview-teju-cole/.

Frank, Søren. *Migration and Literature: Günter Grass, Milan Kundera, Salman Rushdie, and Jan Kjærstad.* New York: Palgrave Macmillan, 1998.

Gikandi, Simon. "Editor's Column: Provincializing English." *PMLA* 129, no. 1 (January 2014): 7-17. https://www.jstor.org/stable/24769418.

———. "Preface." In *Negotiating Afropolitanism: Essays on Borders and Spaces in Contemporary African Literature and Folklore,* edited by Jennifer Wawrizinek and J. K. S. Makokha, 9-12. Amsterdam: Rodopi, 2011.

Goyal, Yogita. "Postcolonialism, Still." *Post45* (*Contemporaries: Forms of the Global Anglophone)*, February 22, 2019. https://post45.org/2019/02/postcolonial-still/.

Guarracino, Serena. "Writing 'so raw and true': Blogging in Chimamanda Ngozi Adichie's *Americanah.*" *Between* 4, no. 8 (November 2014): 1-27. http://doi.org/10.13125/2039-6597/1320.

Mbembe, Achille. "Afropolitanism." In *Africa Remix: Contemporary Art of a Continent,* edited by Simon Njami and Lucy Durán, 26-30. Johannesburg: Jacana, 2007.

———. "The Internet Is Afropolitan." Interview by Bregtje van der Haak. *The Chimurenga Chronic New Cartographies,* August 7, 2015. http://chimurenga chronic.co.za/the internet-is-afropolitan/.

Pahl, Miriam. "Afropolitanism as critical consciousness: Chimamanda Ngozi Adichie's and Teju Cole's internet presence." *Journal of African Cultural Studies* 28, no. 1 (March 2016): 73-87. https://www.jstor.org/stable/24758432.

Said, Edward. "The *Connection* Interview with Edward Said." Interview by Christopher Lydon. *Interviews with Edward Said,* edited by Amritjit Singh and Bruce G. Johnson, 199-219. Jackson: University of Mississippi Press, 2000.

———. *Culture and Imperialism.* New York: Knopf, 1993.

Santana, Stephanie Bosch. "Exorcizing the future: Afropolitanism's spectral origins." *Journal of African Cultural Studies* 28, no. 1 (March 2016): 120-126. https://www.jstor.org/stable/24758438.

Selasi, Taiye. "Bye-Bye Babar." *The Lip Magazine,* March 3, 2005. http://thelip. robertsharp.co.uk/?p=76.

Solés, Gemma. "Wainaina on Afropolitanism." *UrbanAfrica.Net,* April 4, 2014. http://www. urbanafrica.net/urban-voices/wainaina-afropolitanism/.

Wood, James. "Sunjeev Sahota's Novels of Arrival and Departure." *The New Yorker,* August 2, 2021. https://www.newyorker.com/magazine/2021/08/09/sunjeev-sahotas-novels-of-arrival-and-departure.

Section III.
Conclusions

Chapter 7

Decolonial Post45 and America as object of study

Sushil Sivaram

UWC Dilijan College

Abstract

This essay proposes that Post45 cannot become global by simply engaging with non-American writers, texts, and perspectives. The question is not just about geography or even an "imaginative geography." Instead, I suggest that the way to re-frame the discussion and think of the field from a decolonial elsewhere is to ask how and why American intellectual and literary-cultural institutions and discourses (re)instituted plurality, multiplicity, and alterity as key optics to understand the self, explain the "other" to itself, and justify its own dominant position in the cultural-academic field. More specifically, how did it use literature and culture from around the world to stabilize and in turn globalize (and universalize) a discourse about literary culture?

Instead, one possible question that Post-45 should ask is if the American Century rearticulated and made more powerful the intellectual legacy of Orientalism, Western categories, and knowledges, or did it really undermine it. More specifically, how did institutional locations and circuits of knowledge in the U.S. produce some of the most influential explanations of "other" literatures and cultures. The problem I am trying to grapple with here is, how do I not produce only oppositional critique but engage in what Walter Mignolo calls "epistemic disobedience." Disobedience in my case attempts to make the American post-war literary and intellectual field an object of study so that we historicize knowledge production and do not simply reproduce dominant epistemic frameworks.

Keywords: World Literature; Post45; Mignolo, Walter; Multiculturalism; Epistemic Disobedience

***

In 2019, when my apprenticeship in the US academy was coming to an end, I seriously began to question my position inside this institutional location.[1] I knew that this was not a new problem and many generations of foreign and "immigrant" students to the US had grappled with this existential question in their own ways. I had often seen myself as a visitor rather than an immigrant, as if this difference had a political significance and an impact on my identity as a foreigner. But I quickly realized that I felt at home, like a resident, within the academic discourse community of the English Department. The hospitality that this institutional location offered me was limitless and I rarely felt like an outsider. It allowed me to perform a flexible identity where one day I would be an American academic working in a South Asian context, and on the other days, I would inhabit a South Asian mind space and think within those constraints. This flexibility felt both free and evasive, and I thought I should take a stand and represent South Asia. It felt ethical to make the US academy multicultural and worldly through this idea that I embodied a South Asian identity. And yet the more I thought about it, the more I felt that my allegiance was to the academic world, the field that I pursued, and the institutional location that I inhabited. I choose the freedom that the academy offered. But what really were the boundaries of these "field" positions? Did they overlap with national boundaries, the physical location of institutions, the communities they engendered, and the publics they served and reproduced? These were essentially questions that problematized the space and place of knowledge production—and that is why it was also a question about the worlds we inhabit. I often felt that there were no outsides to the social scientific and humanistic enterprise whose main global and transnational location was within the university. I belonged to a discourse community that produced systematic knowledge (science) about literature and literary culture using, producing, and sharing the same norms, codes, and concerns regardless of geographical or national locations. This is what made me wonder if the only option, even now, was to provincialize the Euro-American field because it was universally applicable in Delhi, Dhaka, and D. C. Or were there other ways to think about the world outside the institutional location we occupy?

At the outset, I wish to be clear that, when I speak about knowledge production and systematic knowledge, I am referring to criticism, literary theory, social theory, and the humanities as an academic discipline. I am not referring to the general production of things literary which include extra-academic activities, in print or online, such as book reviews, essays, and commentaries in magazines. These are our objects of study alongside

---

[1] [Editor's note] In 2019, Sushil Sivaram was a PhD candidate in English at Rutgers University.

literature. Academic criticism and humanities education, at least in the US, are predominantly located within the university, and these extra-academic activities belong to their own discourse communities that sometimes, but not always, intersect with the academic community. But this is not a universal fact because literary studies as a discipline is not a universal fact. For instance, one can argue that historically, different kinds of humanities education lay mostly outside the university and in many locations even today, this education takes various forms, ranging from discussion groups that meet around charismatic individuals to events such as Baul (mystic minstrel) festivals, philosophical discussions in and outside religious institutions, conversations in village squares, to passing down knowledge about the arts and literature through music and dance traditions. In comparison to the other social sciences, the literary field still represents linguistic, epistemic, historical, and institutional plurality and this is what opens up the possibilities to recognize and access different worlds, discourse communities, and publics. The capaciousness and in-disciplined nature of the field itself can be generative to think about disciplinary questions like the one this edited collection asks.

An English Department in Sonipat that is structurally like an English department in Stanford, that teaches a similar "multicultural" canon organized around cognate thematic boundaries, and that instructs students to ask similar questions about their objects of study cannot be the right place to start. The outside cannot be just about localizing content or thinking in terms of national and ethnic identities if these specificities get subsumed under a universal way of practicing the humanities and the social sciences. The theoretical crux of the problem is the need to square what seems like "colonial difference" which, according to Walter Mignolo, lies in the "politics of their loci of enunciation" with the overpowering force of our own academic habitus, "a product of history, [that] produces individual and collective practices—more history—in accordance with the schemes generated by history."[2] The argument that I propose in this essay is that we should think about the idea of a "world" in terms of institutions and discourse communities. The question this different optic to community formation raises is whether it is possible to view disciplinary formations in the global academy from outside our own institutional location. If so, where does this outside lie? The conclusion I come to is that this outside is not the freedom of experience, nor the freedom to experience the other, but that the decolonial elsewhere can emerge only out of the absence of the freedom in experience.

---

[2] Walter D. Mignolo, "The Geopolitics of Knowledge and the Colonial Difference," *South Atlantic Quarterly* 101, no. 1 (January 2002): 63, https://doi.org/10.1215/00382876-101-1-57; Pierre Bourdieu, *The Logic of Practice*, trans. Richard Nice (Stanford: Stanford UP, 1990), 54.

My training in the US academy has had its effects. I feel the institutional power structures, the visible and invisible norms, and the values that compel me to take certain positions. To return to the existential question that troubled me in 2019, I always felt that I was forced to locate myself within the academy and speak about my object of study, the literary field in India, from outside it. But, as Pierre Bourdieu writes in the Preface to *Homo Academicus*, the only way to gain a semblance of control over the object of study is to "objectify the objectifying subject."[3] He elaborates:

> It is by turning to study the historical conditions of his own production, rather than by some form or other of transcendental reflection, that the scientific subject can gain a theoretical control over his own structures and inclinations as well as over the determinants whose products they are, and can thereby gain the concrete means of reinforcing his capacity for objectification.[4]

Hence, the "America" in the title of this chapter is a stand-in for both the subject and the institutional location that this subject occupies. And to decolonize a field like Post45 (or even Postcolonial Literature, World Literature, Global Anglophone, etc.) would require us to fold back on our own practices, our ability to theorize, and our need to produce knowledge about the field we study. The question about one's positionality within the field is not new, but my strong belief is that literary scholars must make it a part of their research questions in reflexive ways. This necessity to "objectify the objectifying subject" becomes even more imperative now that we know so well the colonial legacies of our intellectual pursuits and the imperial foundations of our institutions and fields.

*****

In 1991, Robert Young asked Gayatri Spivak about her academic positionality in an interview that he called "Neocolonialism and the Secret Agent of Knowledge." Her answer is still relevant today because it fundamentally troubles the questions this collection asks about Americanist perspectives, disciplinary formations like Post45, the location of the global, alterity, difference, identity, and representation in the academic humanities. Spivak's provocation forces us to ask if Post45 and other new field formations are reproducing a Euro-American-centric paradigm, or whether they are moving towards a more politically engaged decolonial future. It is well established that the oppositional critique to Eurocentrism emerged and was institutionalized within the American academy. But the reasons for this are still not completely

---

[3] Pierre Bourdieu, *Homo Academicus*, trans. Peter Collier (Stanford: Stanford UP, 1988), xxi.

[4] Bourdieu, *Homo Academicus*, xxi.

clear and we cannot claim that a critique of Eurocentrism has been fully successful in dismantling the problems with post-Enlightenment rationalism. Similarly, when disciplines emerge within institutions, say from Commonwealth Literature to Postcolonial Literature to Global Anglophone Literature, or from Comparative Literature to World Literature, scholars cannot assume that they follow a developmental logic that claims that the field is getting better. Rather, it should force us to reflect on older critiques and the power of the automatic institutional processes once they have been set into motion. For example, it was an emancipatory anticolonialism in colonized spaces that ended up becoming institutional postcolonialism, an academic discipline, in Anglo-America where a series of actions, attitudes, research, classroom practices and speech-acts formalized (or instituted) the oppositional ethos into an activity of its own. Besides, Post45 is not a debate occurring in the Indian literary field and I wonder if one should ask why not there in the postcolonial location, and why here, even before we ask how one can think about the field from outside the United States?

In this context, Spivak says something interesting about disciplinary neocolonialism and reflexive methodology in this interview. I want to use her insight as a yardstick to begin to think about this edited collection's goal to re-frame the discussions in Post45 by engaging with non-American writers, texts, and perspectives. Spivak's position interests me because my own argument in this essay is about the larger question of the universality or particularity of the academic humanities and literary studies as a disciplinary formation around the world. The examples I draw on will be predominantly from the US and India. Spivak says that "neocolonialism in general, I'm speaking very broadly, has as its alibi a fully-fledged cultural relativism. Neocolonialism is also interested in fostering rights talk in a class specific situation."[5] Spivak suggests that we like to think that there are local epistemes to draw from, what she calls "identity models that will seem like they are coming from other cultural spaces," but in reality "what…[we] are doing is a travestied Hegel [or bad Enlightenment thinking]."[6] Yes, the emergence of cultural relativism may have been a reaction to the universality espoused by Enlightenment thinking. However, the emergence of a progressive relativism was itself embedded in notions of different identities and the notion of the "other," which in turn was based on discovering distant civilizations, colonialism, empire building, and nation thinking. Historically, the desire to find local epistemes, as Edward Said writes in *Orientalism*, was a way to produce an identity for the self (the

---

[5] Gayatri Chakravorty Spivak, "Neocolonialism and the Secret Agent of Knowledge," *Oxford Literary Review* 13, no. 1 (July 1991): 224, https://www.jstor.org/stable/43973717.

[6] Spivak, "Neocolonialism and the Secret Agent of Knowledge," 225.

"objectifying subject"). This is what I think Spivak means when she says that neocolonialism's alibi is cultural relativism. The key here is to then think beyond identity as the only marker of a local episteme and to understand that the "self" in *Orientalism* was a set of emerging disciplines that would become the bedrock of the modern university.

Additionally, Spivak suggests that the worlding of the world in both metropolitan and postcolonial locations occurs within a certain upper-class (and I will add caste in the case of India) that leaves out the subaltern: for Antonio Gramsci, the proletarian who is structurally not part of the capitalistic bourgeoise (state) narrative, and for Spivak, in the postcolonial context "everything that has limited or no access to cultural imperialism…— a space of difference."[7] Hence asserting a monolithic identity like Indian culture or Indian literature always looks good from the colonial and neocolonial point of view because that is what colonization denies or erases. Simultaneously, metropolitan cultures produce their own literary, cultural, and academic institutional identity in relation to what it denies the colonial and neocolonial spaces. At the same time, Indian culture or Indian literature is also a class preoccupation aligned with nation-building culturalist activities, which is an example of cultural imperialism that elides the subaltern from within the postcolonial space. Some scholars argue that the position of the subaltern has changed in India in the last 30 years because of rapid globalization and economic growth. But to offer a counterargument, Spivak's position still holds true because colonial institutional structures of knowledge production do not follow the same temporal rhythms of the economic world. They have a life of their own and are still being dismantled very slowly and are far from being reassembled. Finally, according to Spivak, the idea of the monolithic other is easier to institutionalize in remote locations because "it leaves the heterogeneity of other spaces aside and produces an easier politically correct brand of cultural studies."[8] These are the lessons that Post45 must learn from its own disciplinary history (like postcolonial studies) when seeking to either globalize or provincialize itself.

Rather than simply critique the US academy's turn towards pluralizing the field by turning to the "world" and the "globe," I feel a return to a document like this allows us to think about how one has reached the current juncture. It lets us reflect on why we turn to specific kinds of texts to make specific arguments

---

[7] Spivak, "Necolonialism and the Secret Agent of Knowledge"; Leon de Kock, "Interview with Gayatri Chakravorty Spivak: New Nation Writers Conference in South Africa," *Ariel: A Review of International English Literature* 23, no. 3 (July 1992): 30-47.

[8] Spivak, "Neocolonialism and the Secret Agent of Knowledge," 226.

(or refuse to engage with them), and forces us to ask if just engaging with those texts, now canonical, is enough to oppose a neo- or a continuing colonialism we feel we are part of. Spivak's position is specific though. For her, this "pathetic kind of multiculturalism" is necessary in the US context as a counter to "white majority racist arguments that humanities education …should be devoted to a study of whatever Western culture is."[9] This is similar to how H. A. R. Gibb rationalized the Orient in the interwar period (1931) when he suggested that the East is useful "to the Western mind in the struggle to overcome narrowness, oppressive specialization, and limited perspectives."[10] The flip side of this necessary act is that "in order to be reactive to the white majority, we have in fact also, because we do not want to be self-critical, to become involved in a new Orientalism as regards other places."[11] But outside of racial and nativist arguments about engaging the other, Spivak does see a truer kind of engagement which is an immersion into the space of difference—the subaltern space—that facilitates the emergence of alternative epistemes. Whether this can be done from within the institutional structures of the academy or not is a moot question; my reading of the interview suggests that this change cannot come from within the academy. It is only by stepping out of our institutional location and discourse communities that we can inhabit this space of difference. That is why Spivak invokes Gayle Omvedt as an exemplar. Omvedt is an American-born and trained academic who moved to India in the late 1970s and became a Dalit/anti-caste activist, researcher, and writer. Following this logic, the others who Spivak would find exemplary are figures like Frantz Fanon, Rigoberta Menchú, Gloria Anzaldúa, Vandana Shiva, Kancha Ilaiah, Abdelkhebir Khatibi, and Édouard Glissant.

The argument is not to go "native," nor is expanding the canon to include more and more identity categories a solution because both are implicated within the logics of cultural imperialism and cultural relativism. However, we still need to keep asking: where is the decolonial elsewhere? There is a problem as soon as our object of study looks like more local detail within the same structural logic Spivak identifies. Rather, we must ask if there are other epistemic traditions, practices, and decolonial elsewheres that need to be heard and allowed to emerge as parallel practices to our own. The question then is where the outside is, or the decolonial elsewhere of Post45, or more broadly, the academic humanities in its global and transnational form. In what follows, I want to engage in two different thought experiments, one about the academic humanities in the US, in a settler colonial framework that inherits,

---

[9] Spivak, "Neocolonialism and the Secret Agent of Knowledge," 227.

[10] Edward Said, *Orientalism* (New York: Pantheon, 1978), 257.

[11] Said, *Orientalism*, 10-11.

builds on, and makes its own the European humanities and social sciences. The second is about academic humanities in a postcolonial location like India, where it first appears as cultural imperialism and hegemony in the late 1800s, but then undergoes intense scrutiny between the 1950s and the 1990s, where it meets up, again and again, with the development of the academic humanities in the US in the post-45 period.

*****

To begin, I turn to the US field and begin with a similar question Zoe Todd (Red River Métis, Otipemisiwak) asks about the field she inhabits: anthropology. Todd begins her polemic with two vignettes, but a short summary of the first will be enough for me to make my point. Todd is listening to Bruno Latour give a talk about climate as a "common cosmopolitical concern" when he refers to the concept of Gaia. This is Todd's reaction to Latour:

> Having just returned from a year of research in the Inuvialuit Settlement Region in Canada's Western Arctic, I was intrigued. Funny, I thought, this sounds an awful lot like the little bit of Inuit cosmological thought and legal orders that I have been taught by Inuit colleagues, friends and teachers [. ...] Surely, I naively thought, if Bruno Latour was referencing Gaia, maybe he would reference Sila, the well-known Inuit concept that is today translated by many non-Inuit as climate but Sila is also 'the breathe [sic] that circulates into and out of every living thing.'[12]

The rest of Todd's essay proceeds as if this epiphany revealed the missing decolonial elsewhere in Latour's position: a space which includes indigenous thinkers, their worldviews, epistemic traditions, and practices as concurrent with the way we (in academia) think about the climate. For Todd and others, the problem is a structural one and a critique of this structure must begin with a critique of the disciplines we inhabit and their institutional locations because "decolonization of thought cannot happen until the proponents of the discipline themselves are willing to engage in the decolonial project in a substantive and structural and physical way, and willing to acknowledge that the colonial is an extant, ongoing reality."[13] The question for literary studies, and more specifically Post45, will be to first acknowledge, identify, and then act upon its colonial and neocolonial impulses regardless of where in the world one is located.

---

[12] Zoe Todd, "An Indigenous Feminist's Take On The Ontological Turn: 'Ontology' Is Just Another Word For Colonialism," *Journal of Historical Sociology* 29, no. 1 (March 2016): 5, https://doi.org/10.1111/johs.12124.

[13] Todd, "An Indigenous Feminist's Take on the Ontological Turn," 17.

The literary field and the humanities more broadly are different from anthropology because the former exists both inside and outside the academy. This difference is important, and I will return to it when I turn to the Indian field. In Todd's paper, the category in question is climate or climate change. What if we replace this with literature or the literary and ask what other worldviews, epistemic traditions, and practices—the decolonial elsewhere— can the humanities engage with at the structural level? Can this decolonial elsewhere emerge from within the academy? Probably not. I want to suggest that these methods of engaging the literary are out in the public sphere, in what people do. This I think is a markedly different operation than pluralizing the field from within the academy where Indigenous Studies, Native American Literature, Ethnic Studies, South Asian Studies, etc. are sub-disciplines within the still colonial and neo-oriental structures of the humanities and social sciences that still function on the premise of a problematic cultural relativism among other things. Todd is not alone in thinking this today, and, closer to our own discipline, Walter Mignolo calls it the colonial difference that engenders "border thinking…an epistemology from the subaltern's perspective."[14] What I am suggesting is that the colonial difference is revealed in assuming that literary studies or the academic humanities (the fields we occupy) are universal disciplines that can be replicated in other intellectual and epistemic locations. Or colonial difference is revealed when we ask if we can pluralize the discipline by including more and more voices from ethnic, racial, geographical, and national locations without stepping out of the structures of the fields and disciplines we inhabit.

Therefore, literary studies in India that are fashioned after the older British system or a newer American liberal arts model are not really stepping out of the colonial and neocolonial structures of the academic humanities. Once we begin to think about the "world" in terms of institutions and discourse communities, we cannot argue what or who is Indian, British, or American based on national or ethnic identities. The norms of the institution and the members of the institution who produce and reproduce those norms are ideally defined by an allegiance to a different cause, in this case, the production of systematic knowledge. Hence, a more generative way to think of difference that really matters would be to think of it in terms of institutional habits and norms. Spivak concurs with this position in the interview with Robert Young when he asks her if transporting deconstruction to India is neocolonialist? This her reply: "[Y]ou see this is what I was thinking about in terms of this spurious kind of production of models of identity. One can say I am Roman, I am an Indian, I am Alexander, when in fact, the way of thinking is colored by the last

---

[14] Mignolo, "The Geopolitics of Knowledge and the Colonial Difference," 71.

two centuries of exchange."[15] Spivak points to the notion that the way we organize our concepts and theories about the world, about pluralism, and about imaginative geography are a product of socially constituted practices and institutional norms that emerged and developed in collusion with the imperialism and colonialism of the last 200 years. What, then, could be the outside of cultural imperialism, or the decolonial elsewhere in the US and in India? How do we begin to "objectify the objectifying subject?" I will offer three possibilities, but I can only hope that epistemic futures like these are possible. The examples are attempts by others who have come close to locating and inhabiting this decolonial elsewhere.

*****

My understanding is that the decolonial elsewhere could function in the following ways. I will frame all these possibilities as questions. What if we keep historicizing and locating the dominant global colonial and neocolonial (what we used to call Euro-American) academic discourses in the US and in India? Or as Spivak puts it, we must continue to attend to "the way of thinking" that "is colored by the last two centuries of exchange."[16] In other words, we must make the American post-war literary and intellectual field or Post45 itself an object of study. I feel this could be a way to self-reflexively understand one's own intellectual habits and dispositions, or habitus, in different social contexts. An example of this could be a study of sub-disciplines (postcolonial studies, south Asian studies), academic departments (South Asian Languages and Civilizations at the University of Chicago), events (the Annual Conference on South Asia at the University of Wisconsin, Madison), organizations (South Asian Literary Association), and journals to understand their rationale. I am drawing on an insight from Pierre Bourdieu and Loïc Wacquant to ask if their sociological method can become a decolonial tool to rigorously situate the knowledge we produce and employ. For instance, Bourdieu and Wacquant write:

> [...] if it is true that the dehistoricization that almost inevitably results from the migration of ideas across national boundaries is one of the factors contributing to derealization and false universalization (as, for example, with theoretical '*faux amis*'), then only a genuine history of the genesis of ideas about the social world, combined with an analysis of the social mechanisms of the international circulation of those ideas, could lead intellectuals, in this domain as elsewhere, to a better mastery of

---

[15] Spivak, "Neocolonialism and the Secret Agent of Knowledge," 232-233.
[16] Spivak, "Neocolonialism and the Secret Agent of Knowledge," 232-233.

those instruments with which they argue without taking the trouble to argue beforehand about them.[17]

In other words, to historicize Post45 and make it an object of study may be a way to reveal the cunning of imperialist reason, while at the same time remaining aware of the institutional impulses that drive our work. This position also opens the possibility of truly interdisciplinary research where English Departments could collaborate with scholars from History, Sociology, and Anthropology to enquire into each other's disciplinary epistemologies.

The second possibility would be similar to Walter Mignolo's idea of submitting the social sciences and the humanities to a "double movement of appropriation and radical criticism from the perspective of the indigenous to the point of revealing the colonial difference."[18] In India, first, we will have to be open to learning from and interacting with subaltern and indigenous knowledges, even if they appear irrational, unfamiliar, and uneasy, because in these very affects lies an inherent critique of what we think to be normative and canonical. Here I am also thinking of Colombian sociologist and decolonial thinker Orlando Fals Borda's work, which suggests that a move like this "can induce independence among intellectuals in poorer nations, as inside observers and actors who are more fully in charge of their own ways and means."[19] As Borda's participatory action research (PAR) demands, research and any kind of action should be done *with* the people and not *for*, *on*, or *about* them. What would literary studies, or research on the literary look like if it is to be done *with* the people? For one, any questions about the use and purpose of literary and cultural studies would disappear. But who are these people and does this question emerge out of a sense of responsibility towards epistemic egalitarianism? In what follows, my third possibility, I will focus mostly on examples from India to show that in addition to dismantling colonial and imperial exchange, systematic knowledge production in South Asia, and a worldly position on Post45 (or Postcolonial Literature, World Literature, the Global Anglophone, etc.) must consider other kinds of power structures and hierarchies in the world. In India, this is the naturalization of caste into the structures of institutions that produce systematic knowledge.

---

[17] Pierre Bourdieu and Loïc Wacquant, "On the Cunning of Imperialist Reason," *Theory, Culture & Society* 16, no. 1 (February 1999): 50-51, https://doi.org/10.1177/026327699016 001003.

[18] Mignolo, "The Geopolitics of Knowledge and the Colonial Difference," 74.

[19] Orlando Fals Borda and Luis E. Mora-Osejo, "Context and Diffusion of Knowledge: A Critique of Eurocentrism," *Action Research* 1, no. 1 (July 2003): 32.

The hierarchies of power and identity groups in the Indian subcontinent are layered differently.[20] Just listing as many, and often overlapping, identity categories that come to my mind randomly—religions, sects, *varna*, *jati*, languages, dialects, tribes, class, gender, etc.—suggests that South Asia is a limit case for something like identity thinking. Therefore, more identity categories in an already plural context do not necessarily offer a solution. But how was and is intellectual and symbolic power distributed in this plural landscape? Dalit scholar Gopal Guru's 2002 provocation, in the *Economic and Political Weekly*, called "Egalitarianism and the Social Sciences in India" identifies one of the most prominent intellectual fault lines by showing that the structural advantage of doing theoretical work in India lies with the "top of the twice born (TTB)," or the upper-caste Brahmins. There is a reason for this, and I paraphrase and interpret Guru, who writes that the epistemic closure is sanctioned at the originary point, in mythology, and in codified texts. The constant redistribution of Manu's codes denies learning, or even the mind, to Dalits and women because they are born from the feet of the creator.[21] This is the basis for a pseudo-religious and pseudo-mythic justification for an Indian caste and racial theory. According to Guru, religion and social practices naturalize this into folk consciousness.[22] But at the same time, he extends this naturalization to the modern social-scientific establishment and the academy in India. The problem is not often with individuals (though it can be that too), but with structures that organize and distribute resources to societies. That is why, by pointing to what is an essentialist and mythical understanding of identity, Guru suggests that a different genealogy to power has an effect in the organization of the Indian social and intellectual world at a structural level.

In additional to the 200 years of colonial and imperial exchange, systematic knowledge production in South Asia must consider the naturalization of caste hierarchies at the structural level. Guru's critique offers a way to think about the nested nature (from local to global) of the problem because theorizing Dalit experience is a social necessity for the Dalit subject to escape the object

---

[20] See Tuhiwai Linda Smith, *Decolonializing Methodologies: Research and Indigenous People* (Dudein: University of Otago Press, 2001), 7. The term "indigenous" does not have the same valence in India as it does in settler colonies. "Indigenous'' as a term emerged in the US in the 70s out of the American Indian Movement (AIM) and the Canadian Indian Brotherhood movement that was later internationalized.

[21] Manu, or the first man in South Asian mythology is the author of the *Manusmriti*, or the Law of Manu. The *Manusmriti* codifies and rationalizes all forms of inequality (caste, gender and economic). It is the ur-anti-social mobility treatise produced.

[22] Gopal Guru, "Egalitarianism and the Social Sciences in India," in *The Cracked Mirror: An Indian Debate on Experience and Theory* (Oxford: Oxford UP, 2017), 16.

position and the "empirical mode" they have existed in thus far. In other words, by questioning the source texts, and the structural underpinnings of institutions (a curious mix of local and colonial logics), the Dalit subject becomes independent of the gaze of a particular kind of researcher (high caste, Western, or culturally distant). And as Fals Borda shows in a different context, these subjects become "inside observers and actors" in control of their own "ways and means."

Hence, Guru insists that the theorization of Dalit experience, an alternate genealogy to power, and decolonial thought can only emerge out of the lived experience and epistemological positions of Dalits. Rather than dismiss this as an essentialism, I believe that this claim should be taken seriously because it is the only way to interact with parallel subjugated, subaltern, and indigenous experiences and knowledges. In the absence of this standpoint, Guru identifies at least three dangers, or "reverse orientalism[s]," where the structural relationship between the patron and the client who is in need of "epistemological charity" remains intact and replicates the "Brahmanical mechanism of first controlling knowledge resources and then pouring them into the empty cupped palms of the Dalits."[23] Second, when non-Dalits theorize from outside Dalit experience, it "fails to explain who has arrived—whether the object (Dalits) or the subject (researchers)."[24] Guru calls this a "posterior epistemology," the standpoint of which does not emerge from Dalit experience, but from "critiques of mainstream Marxist or feminist framework."[25] Falling back on the "mainstream," rather than experience, is an example of the institutional nature of the problem. Marxism and feminism are too entrenched in the system now and this is counterproductive because Dalit marginalization is not simply an academic question, it is a cultural and political project for self-determination. That is also why any kind of egalitarian ambition for the humanities and the social sciences must be a bottom-up, rather than a top-down, project. Therefore, for Guru, turning "Dalit epistemology into an exegetical horizon of difference," a reading practice, or a pedagogy undermines the whole project.[26] This is anti-institutional and questions the institutionalization of difference exactly like Spivak does in the earlier example; stepping out of our institutional locations and discourse communities is one way to inhabit difference. Practically, this would mean that just teaching the Dalit literary corpus in Indian or American classrooms cannot be the way to engage the decolonial elsewhere. It must go beyond by somehow showing how the privileged can facilitate, not help, other forms and types of knowledge to emerge. This can only happen when we begin

---

[23] Guru, "Egalitarianism and the Social Sciences in India," 25.

[24] Guru, "Egalitarianism and the Social Sciences in India," 26.

[25] Guru, "Egalitarianism and the Social Sciences in India," 26-27.

[26] Guru, "Egalitarianism and the Social Sciences in India," 27.

to "objectify the objectifying subject," as Bourdieu tells us. What I also have in mind is a type of humanities or humanistic social activism and social work. This is because, in Guru's model, the structurally dominant can never speak for the dominated, however well-meaning the dominant is. We can reject this and keep doing what we do, or we can take Guru seriously. Philosopher Sunder Sarukkai does exactly this: he takes Guru seriously.

For Sarukkai, the crux of Guru's position and argument lies in the difference between lived experience and experience, or between "the experience of *being* a subject and not an experience *by* a subject or about a subject."[27] Rather than teach or study the Baul tradition and its songs or tribal and indigenous stories in a classroom via methods like close reading or textual analysis, one would have to approach the notion of the literary itself from within a Baul or tribal and indigenous cosmological and epistemic point of view. This is not something that is essentialist, but rather framed through their practices, belief systems, and ways of living in this world. It would mean that we become Baul. And the way to do this may not be to simply "research" or "read" about the Baul, but to become them without an exit strategy. Without this commitment, the subject-object duality will always remain.

Can work like this exist within the structures of the university? And why is this important? One reason is that the logic of producing the kind of theory Guru speaks about is not about the freedom to experience other cultures, cosmologies, and epistemologies. In layman's terms, that is the logic behind the idea of tourism and orientalism—and they have their advantages and disadvantages. Rather, as Sarukkai puts it, "*lived experience is not about freedom of experience but about the lack of freedom in an experience.*"[28] To extrapolate, imperialism, colonialism and neocolonialism, casteism, and racial hierarchy are all positions of power that are embedded with this privilege of the "freedom of experience," while the decolonial elsewhere must emerge out of the "lack of freedom in an experience."

*****

I want to conclude with an example of an alternative that I believe takes the question of the decolonial elsewhere in India seriously via the idea of a humanities or humanistic social activism and social work. The Bhasha Research and Publication Center and the Adivasi Academy started by G. N. Devy and

---

[27] Sunder Sarukkai, "Experience and Theory: From Habermas to Gopal Guru," in *The Cracked Mirror: An Indian Debate on Experience and Theory* (Oxford: Oxford UP, 2017), 36, italics in original.

[28] Sarukkai, "Experience and Theory," 36.

others do not attempt to bring tribal languages, oral literatures, and practices into the classroom, but works with the community to produce social and cultural infrastructures where their epistemologies can continue to survive and make sense of the modernity of which they are now a part.[29] This is a little like Fals Borda's Participatory Action Research (PAR) and Mignolo's border thinking. Devy's project is not theoretical, nor is it pedagogical. It does not exist only in the realm of ideas; it ventures out into the materiality of difficult spaces, both intellectual and corporeal. And most importantly, it does not display a desire or wish to understand the other, scientifically, anthropologically, or sociologically. Rather, it is a way to have a conversation with the community about how one sees and explains the worlds we inhabit. For instance, Devy writes that the Adivasi Academy teaches "young men and women of the area a subject that we have named 'Tribal Studies,' by which we mean 'the study and understanding of how the Adivasis perceive the world.' The attempt is to make our students reflect on their own situation, motivate them and to put them onto the great task of empowering the Adivasi villages by helping them to be self-reliant."[30]

So, to return to the questions of the outside of the institutions we inhabit and uphold, the world for Post45, and other such disciplinary formations, I feel that this outside can only emerge when we begin to question our academic subjectivity and ask how we know what we know and why we legitimate our versions of truth so passionately. At a less metaphysical level, I think the problem in different geographical locations, in different social milieus, and in different institutional locations will be different because the interacting social variables, knowledges, and habitus will always be different. At the same time, I feel that decolonizing Post45, literary studies, or the academic humanities more broadly is only one aspect of the problem—and this may be more acute in the American context where institutional criticism and knowledge production is a fairly robust establishment. In the Indian context, one first needs to ask how successful and widespread institutional criticism and literary knowledge production is, and, if it really is not as well entrenched as in other locations like the US, then ask how else we can rethink and collaborate with the outside, now that we know to some extent what the inside feels like.

Works cited

Bourdieu, Pierre. *Homo Academicus*. Translated by Peter Collier. Stanford: Stanford UP, 1988.

---

[29] Ganesh N. Devy, "Culture and Development, an Experiment with Empowerment," *Field Actions Science Reports* 7 (2013): 1-7, https://journals.openedition.org/factsreports/2404.

[30] Devy, "Culture and Development," 5.

———. *The Logic of Practice*. Translated by Richard Nice. Stanford: Stanford UP, 1990.

———, and Loïc Wacquant. "On the Cunning of Imperialist Reason." *Theory, Culture & Society* 16, no. 1 (February 1999): 41-58. https://doi.org/10.1177/02 6327699016001003.

Devy, Ganesh N. "Culture and Development, an Experiment with Empowerment." *Field Actions Science Reports* 7 (2013): 1-7. http://journals.openedition.org/factsreports/2404.

Fals Borda, Orlando, and Luis E. Mora-Osejo. "Context and Diffusion of Knowledge: A Critique of Eurocentrism." *Action Research* 1, no. 1 (July 2003): 29-37.

Guru, Gopal. "Egalitarianism and the Social Sciences in India." In *The Cracked Mirror: An Indian Debate on Experience and Theory*, 9-28. Oxford: Oxford UP, 2017.

de Kock, Leon. "Interview with Gayatri Chakravorty Spivak: New Nation Writers Conference in South Africa." *Ariel: A Review of International English Literature* 23, no. 3 (July 1992): 30-47.

Mignolo, Walter D. "The Geopolitics of Knowledge and the Colonial Difference." *South Atlantic Quarterly* 101, no. 1 (January 2002): 57-96. https://doi.org/10.1215/00382876-101-1-57.

Said, Edward. *Orientalism*. New York: Pantheon, 1978.

Sarukkai, Sunder. "Experience and Theory: From Habermas to Gopal Guru." In *The Cracked Mirror: An Indian Debate on Experience and Theory*, 29-45. Oxford: Oxford UP, 2017.

Smith, Tuhiwai Linda. *Decolonializing Methodologies: Research and Indigenous People*. Dudein: University of Otago Press, 2001.

Spivak, Gayatri Chakravorty. "Neocolonialism and the Secret Agent of Knowledge." *Oxford Literary Review* 13, no. 1 (July 1991): 220-251. https://www.jstor.org/stable/43973717.

Todd, Zoe. "An Indigenous Feminist's Take On The Ontological Turn: 'Ontology' Is Just Another Word For Colonialism." *Journal of Historical Sociology* 29, no. 1 (March 2016): 4-22. https://doi.org/10.1111/johs.12124.

Coda.
"We will make our own future text"

William G. Welty

Rutgers, The State University of New Jersey

Abstract

This brief coda contextualizes the arguments and concerns of the collection within recent history, focusing especially on the Post45 response to the Trump era of American history.

Keywords: Post45 Group; Trump, Donald; Reed, Ishmael; COVID

***

In early 2019, Marina Bilbija, writing in *Post45*, contextualized Global Anglophone studies within the violent post-Trump and post-Brexit moment. That was also the moment when I began working on this collection in earnest. Her thoughts offer both a glimpse of the global context in which this manuscript began to take shape and a chance to re-contextualize the preceding essays in the years that have passed since. She wonders:

> What does it mean to 'do' Global Anglophone Studies at a time when an ordinary conversation in Spanish in a New York restaurant could propel a customer into such a fit of rage that he would threaten to call ICE on the spot? The fact that scenes like this are also being reported in the post-Brexit UK indicate a resurgent violent and racist investment in the category of the English speaker on both sides of the Atlantic. What do these things have in common: an emergent, new field of English literary studies, and a white American rejecting Spanish-speakers as possible fellow-citizens? On the most basic level, both emphasize Anglophone belonging over other forms of local, regional, or identity-based affiliation.[1]

---

[1] Marina Bilbija, "What's in a Name?: the Global Anglophone, the Anglosphere, and the English-Speaking Peoples," *Post45* (*Contemporaries: Forms of the Global Anglophone*), February 22, 2019, https://post45.org/2019/02/whats-in-a-name-the-global-anglophone-the-anglosphere-and-the-english-speaking-peoples/.

Unfortunately, the questions Bilbija poses have only seemed to gain more urgency in the past years, with a rise in violent racism against Asian-Americans, the murder of George Floyd and countless other African Americans at the hands of the police, the millions dead as a result of COVID, and the ever-worsening catastrophe of global climate change. What does it mean to offer global perspectives on the contemporary in such a moment?

This collection doesn't pretend to offer answers, though it hopes to have formulated some useful questions. While recognizing the pervasive opposition between "Anglophone belonging" and "other forms of [...] affiliation," this collection wonders about the affiliations that might emerge *within and in spite of* that belonging: from the connections of a quintessential text and the Soviet film industry to the competing multilingual paratexts within a work of world literature; from a debate about when and what the contemporary is to the new tellings of migrant journeys within that contemporary. Indeed, the previous chapter takes affiliation and belonging, and their shifting oppositions, parallels, and connections, precisely as its object of study. In formulating those questions—in dwelling on the possibilities of affiliation and belonging in a global, post-45 world—the collection is focused on the now and is also oriented towards the future.

And in thinking of the future, I conclude by returning to Ishmael Reed, whose novel *Mumbo Jumbo* provides the epigraph for this collection. In the early days of the COVID pandemic, I was forcefully struck by the clear and startling parallel between that novel's present and ours. On one hand, *Mumbo Jumbo*'s villains use the Jes' Grew pandemic as a way to try to destroy everything that is threateningly different: the non-white, the non-"American," the non-rational. But on the other, I take heart in the ways that the novel's protagonists, Papa LaBas and Black Herman, try to find liberation and togetherness in the very conditions exposed by Jes' Grew. People read more books and overrun the New York Public Library. They learn about the US history of imperialism in Haiti. They rewrite the history of the world. They come together to help each other, to reflect on the past, and to try to change the future. "We will make our own future text," Papa LaBas says towards the end of the novel.[2]

None of this should detract from the real hurt that is spreading through our world right now. One of the main points of *Mumbo Jumbo* is that reading *cannot* replace attention to the material suffering around us, and the systems that make that suffering possible. But we can learn a little bit from Jes' Grew and *Mumbo Jumbo*: that even in dark times, there are opportunities for learning and growth; for mutual support; for solidarity.

---

[2] Ishmael Reed, *Mumbo Jumbo* (New York: Scribner, 1996), 204.

"We will make our own future text," says Papa LaBas. This text has taken over three years to complete, so the "future" named within it has continually become the present, allowing for a new future to emerge. As the contemporary continues to drift, that process will be ongoing. And yet, sooner or later, that future—that truly global contemporary—will be now.

Works Cited

Bilbija, Marina. "What's in a Name?: the Global Anglophone, the Anglosphere, and the English-
Speaking Peoples." *Post45* (*Contemporaries: Forms of the Global Anglophone*), February 22, 2019. https://post45.org/2019/02/whats-in-a-name-the-global-anglophone-the-anglosphere-and-the-english-speaking-peoples/.

Reed, Ishmael. *Mumbo Jumbo*. New York: Scribner, 1996.

About the contributors

Michael Maguire-Khan has published articles in *American Literature, Criticism, Post45,* and *Critique.* He teaches high school English in Miami.

Amanda Lagji is Assistant Professor of English and World Literature at Pitzer College. Her research interests include postcolonial literature, critical time studies, and terrorism and literature. She publishes widely on postcolonial literature, including recent chapters in *Transnational Africana Women's Fictions* (2021), *Women Writing Diaspora: Transnational Perspectives in the 21st Century* (2021), *The Oxford Handbook of Transnational Law* (2021), and *Timescapes of Waiting: Spaces of Stasis, Delay and Deferral* (2019). Her book, *Postcolonial Fiction and Colonial Time: Waiting for Now* is forthcoming from Edinburgh University Press.

Dan Malinowoski is a PhD candidate at Rutgers University. His dissertation considers how experimental poets react to financialization and the end of the media, specifically at the end of the twentieth century.

Daria Goncharova is a PhD candidate in English at the University of Kentucky, with a background in Linguistics and Cultural Studies. She received her Bachelor's degree in Linguistics from the Southern Federal University, Russia in 2015 and her Master's degree in English from the University of Kentucky in 2018. Her research interests include twentieth-century American literature and film, gender and women's studies, citizenship studies, and critical studies of whiteness. Her dissertation, *Spaces of Citizenship*, explores the role that suburbia played in the cultural negotiation of American citizenship in film and literature of the early Cold War.

Cathryn Piwinski is a current PhD candidate in the English Department at Rutgers University, where she works on twentieth- and twenty-first-century US fiction, book history, and reception theory. She has published with the University of Leiden's *TXT Magazine* and has a co-written book chapter on science fiction TV fan communities forthcoming from Routledge. She is the current Vice President of the James Joyce Society.

Pritika Pradhan received her PhD at the Department of Literatures in English at Rutgers, the State University of New Jersey, in 2019. Her research interests include nineteenth-century British literature, art history, and aesthetic philosophy, and their reincarnations in contemporary literature and culture. She is the recipient of a Raritan Fellowship and Mellon Summer Research Awards from Rutgers University and the Andrew W. Mellon Foundation. Her article on the details of John Ruskin's Gothic aesthetics is forthcoming in *English Literary History* (ELH), and her essay on A. S. Byatt's novel Possession has been accepted for the forthcoming *The Palgrave Handbook of Neo-Victorianism.*

Sushil Sivaram currently lives in Dilijan, Armenia where he is exploring the Caucasus, and working on independent academic and creative writing projects. His scholarly work has appeared in *Comparative Literature, Economic and Political Weekly,* and *Post45.* His creative work has appeared in *Almost Island, Retort Magazine, Lantern Review: A Journal of Asian American Poetry,* and *REAL- Regarding Arts and Letters,* among others. He holds an MFA in poetry from Oklahoma State University and a PhD in Literature from Rutgers University.

William G. Welty earned his PhD in English at Rutgers University in 2020. His writing has appeared in *Politics/Letters, Textual Practice, Hypercultura,* and *Psychoanalysis, Culture, and Society.* He has also contributed chapters to *The Encyclopedia of the Black Arts Movement, Trump Fiction,* and *Creoles, Diasporas, and Cosmopolitanisms.* He lives in New Jersey with his wife, son, and dog.

A collection like this always has more contributors than just the ones mentioned above. Special thanks to all of them, especially the following: the audience members at NeMLA who heard many of these essays in their initial presentation form; the anonymous peer reviewer, for their kind and insightful comments; the staff at Vernon, who believed in this project from the beginning; and Valerie Park-Welty, who believed in both the book and the editor struggling to put it together.

Index

www.ingramcontent.com/pod-product-compliance
Lightning Source LLC
Chambersburg PA
CBHW050520280326
41932CB00014B/2388